PARLIAMENTARY DEMOCRACY IN CANADA

ISSUES *FOR* REFORM

THOMAS D'AQUINO   G. BRUCE DOERN   CASSANDRA BLAIR

162925734

Methuen *Toronto   New York   London   Sydney   Auckland*

CANADIAN CATALOGUING IN PUBLICATION DATA

D'Aquino, Thomas, 1941-
    Parliamentary democracy in Canada

Includes bibliography.
ISBN 0-458-96290-2

1. Canada. Parliament.   2. Canada - Politics and government.   I. Doern, G. Bruce, 1942-   II. Blair, Cassandra.   III. Title.

JL136.D3   328.71   C83-098719-3

ISBN 0-458-96290-2

Editorial and project coordination by Ampersand Publishing Services Inc.

Design by Artplus Design.

Typesetting by Linotext Inc.

Printed and bound in Canada by Les Editions Marquis
1   2   3   4   5   88   87   86   85   84   83

CONTENTS

III
SENATE REFORM AND REGIONAL REPRESENTATION 101

FOREWORD

In terms of our national life, no issue touches us as Canadians more fundamentally than how we are governed. In this respect we are among the world's most fortunate peoples. We enjoy a parliamentary democracy that is basically strong and fair. We are served by institutions that are in large part the envy of the world. However, these conditions have caused us to become complacent, almost casual, in our attitudes toward our political system and the organization and process which sustain it.

The institution of Parliament is the heart of our system of parliamentary democracy. Increasingly, it is coming under fire for its seeming ineffectiveness and lack of relevance. Parliament and its reform is, consequently, the subject of growing interest.

Parliamentary reform was the subject of an earlier study undertaken by the Business Council on National Issues. That study was published in 1979 under the title "Parliamentary Government in Canada: A Critical Assessment and Suggestions for Change." It addressed a wide range of subjects, but focussed particularly on parliamentary theory and practice, question of accountability, and Parliament's legislative role.

The 1979 study was well received by many parliamentarians, other recognized authorities and many interested Canadians. Indeed, the level of continuing interest in the work of the Business Council prompted the preparation of the revised analysis which is the subject of this text. Much of the same ground covered by the original study is again covered here. Considering the importance and timeliness of the national dialogue on Senate reform, a section of this important subject has been added.

The background, terms of reference and organization, and

approach taken on the original study are restated in the Introduction so that readers will understand the nature of the Business Council's initiative then and now. The objectives in this revised study remain the same.

Since publication of the 1979 study, the Business Council on National Issues and and the authors have consulted widely with parliamentarians and others involved in parliamentary government. This revised work reflects their views and experience as well as the opinions and knowledge of those interviewed for the original work. Both the Business Council and the authors hope this new work will continue to provoke reasoned discussion among those who recognize how important it is to have parliamentary institutions that are responsive to the needs of Canadians.

The continuing efforts of the Business Council on National Issues in this area of study so important to our national life would not have been possible without the dedicated leadership provided by the Task Force on Government Organization chaired, in 1979, by Steele Curry, President of Revelstoke Companies Limited, and in 1982, by Warren Chippindale, Chairman and Chief Executive Partner, Coopers & Lybrand. Likewise, the Business Council's ongoing study of our parliamentary institutions would not have been possible without the valuable assistance of the many parliamentarians, public servants and academics who are genuinely committed to the study and achievement of change.

Special acknowledgement has been earned by Peter Vivian, Senior Associate of the Business Council on National Issues, who supervised the preparation of the 1983 study; by Ed Matheson of Ampersand, who edited the manuscript and co-ordinated the design and publication of the project; and by Catherine Spencer of the Business Council staff who typed the manuscript.

Thomas d'Aquino
President

INTRODUCTION

In June, 1978, the Business Council on National Issues (BCNI) commissioned a study of certain aspects of parliamentary government in Canada. That initiative derived from a concern shared by many Canadians, including parliamentarians and respected observers of the legislative process, about the ability of Parliament and the Canadian parliamentary system of government to conduct the nation's affairs effectively. At the heart of that concern were growing misgivings about Parliament's capacity to exact accountability from the government and to provide a credible vehicle for the efficient development of policies and legislation in response to the country's needs. These two areas of concern— accountability and legislative effectiveness—were the focus of the inquiry.

It is reasonable to ask why the Business Council (an organization composed of the chief executive officers of some 150 of Canada's leading companies) chose to examine a subject regarded by some parliamentarians and public servants as the exclusive preserve of government itself. The answer lies in the Business Council's perceptions of government—perceptions shared by most Canadians —that our political institutions are the creation of the people and that those institutions are meant to provide for responsible political leadership in a process in which laws are developed democratically. Within this process, individuals and organizations have a critical role to play as well as a grave responsibility to ensure that the system of government is responsive, accountable and adaptable. It should also encourage respect for the political process and its practitioners. Without such a commitment, government is weakened, the political process becomes the subject of public cynicism and scorn, and the foundations of political legitimacy are undermined. The initiative which led to this study underlines the Business Council's commitment to the strengthening of the Canadian system of government.

The authors undertook their enquiry with the fundamental assumption that the parliamentary form of government has served Canada well and that as a system of government it is both sound and appropriate to Canada's present needs. However, the authors also believe that, despite its many inherent strengths, the system is urgently in need of adaptation if it is to discharge its responsibilities properly and evolve as an effective foundation for democratic government in the future.

Terms of Reference and Organization

The terms of reference for this study are to assess the effectiveness of parliamentary government in Canada with particular focus on major problem areas, and to outline, selectively, some recommendations for change.

The overall objective of the study is to provide both Parliament and the people of Canada with analyses and recommendations that will stimulate public discussion and serve as a catalyst in the urgent task of reappraising parliamentary government in Canada.

Attempts at reform from within Parliament in the recent past have met with only limited success despite the fact that many of the ideas for reform developed by members of Parliament were both desirable and feasible. The authors therefore recognize that achieving a consensus for reform among parliamentarians is an extraordinarily difficult task.

Approach

The approach to the preparation of this study combined research of published and unpublished literature, including parliamentary proceedings and reports. There was also consultation with over 100 individuals who are knowledgeable about parliamentary government.

Consultations were held primarily with active federal parliamentarians and included representatives of the major parties in both the House of Commons and the Senate. In addition, the authors sought the opinions of a number of former parliamentarians whose long and distinguised careers enabled them to address the subject of parliamentary reform with a measure of objectivity and practical wisdom.

Although the focus of research in this study is on the federal Parliament, the authors benefited from the viewpoints of provincial parliamentarians as well. Several provincial premiers, with long experience in provincial legislatures, were among them.

Senior public servants were also consulted. Among these were a number of deputy ministers whose experience with the federal parliamentary process provided the authors with invaluable perspectives, particularly with respect to the complex subject of accountability.

Outside government circles, more limited consultations were held with selected representatives of the private sector, including members of the academic community and the media.

The constraints of time required that the authors identify and select with care the general subject areas to be covered and the specific issues to be given special consideration. The result, therefore, is a study which is thorough in terms of its examination of significant and interrelated issues for public discussion; it is not exhaustive, however.

The present work is indended to encourage positive interest on the part of more Canadians in the vital issue of how we are governed. It was prepared in the belief that constructive public concern about the health of parliamentary government in Canada can help overcome (what have proved to be) two formidable barriers to reform: the failure of citizens to let their elected representatives know *precisely* the nature and urgency of their discontent with the present system; and the partisan conflicts that have, until now, prevented parliamentarians from implementing reform from within.

Ideally, this study will contribute to discussion and debate and serve as a catalyst in the urgent task of reappraising parliamentary government in Canada.

THE NATURE OF PARLIAMENTARY GOVERNMENT IN CANADA

IN ASSESSING PARLIAMENTARY GOVERNMENT in Canada, it is helpful to begin with a consideration of three factors: first, the degree to which general agreement exists concerning the fundamental principles of parliamentary democracy (theory); second, the degree to which the Canadian experience represents a departure from these principles (practice) and; third, the reasons for this discrepancy.

An understanding of these factors and an appreciation of the strengths and weaknesses of parliamentary government make it possible to discuss parliamentary reform constructively and to reconcile, at least in part, general theory and Canadian practice.

Traditional Concepts of Parliamentaray Government in Canada

OBJECTIVES OF PARLIAMENTARY GOVERNMENT

Constitutional authorities and most practising parliamentarians agree that the broad objectives of the parliamentary system of government are:

- to create and support governments in the House of Commons through the support of parliamentary majorities organized along party lines;
- to have a government govern responsibly by allowing it to play a leading role in initiating and formulating policy;
- to develop laws by requiring governments to present and defend their proposals openly in Parliament and to subject all draft legislation and proposals to test, analysis and criticism;

1

- to have open government—and to prevent clandestine government—particularly in the policy-making and administrative spheres;
- to represent and debate the views of citizens and to educate the electorate; and
- in the extreme, to defeat governments and to force their resignations or the dissolution of Parliament.

These objectives are common to parliamentary forms of government throughout the world and are based on the following underlying principles:

1. Cabinet-parliamentary government
2. Ministerial responsibility
3. Public service accountability and neutrality
4. The independence of the judiciary under the rule of law
5. The government's responsibility to govern
6. The right of the House of Commons to withhold financial support
7. The right of the government to initiate money bills
8. The right of individual members of parliament to initiate legislation, resolve grievances, and represent their constituents.

1. Cabinet-Parliamentary Government

The classical Westminster model of parliamentary government exists in the United Kingdom and is based on the principle that responsibility for government rests with the representatives of the people who comprise the majority in the elected assembly. Ministers are chosen by the prime minister, who is either the acknowledged leader of the political party with the largest number of members in the assembly, or, the leader who can win and retain the confidence of the majority of the assembly members. The system is also based on a limited constitutional monarchy with sovereignty residing formally in the Crown. The sovereign retains a limited but nonetheless critical position in the operation of the system in terms of transfer of power and in the exercise, through the cabinet, of limited executive prerogatives.

The prime minister and his appointed ministers constitute the cabinet. Collectively, ministers are responsible for the policies of the government; individually, each minister is responsible for the policy and administration of his department. Public servants are

2

accountable to ministers and advise them on policy. They also have a duty to warn ministers about problems and to execute policy.

The prime minister and the cabinet (and technically, the sovereign) comprise the executive branch of government. However, the term "executive" is often used loosely to include not only the cabinet but also the senior policy advisers (deputy heads of departments, for example) and sometimes the entire federal civil service, which is responsive to the direction of cabinet. The legislative branch of government is Parliament—the sovereign, the Senate and the House of Commons. Simply stated, the role of the legislative branch is to pass laws although it must be understood that "law" is established elsewhere as well. For instance, officials in the executive branch enact subordinate delegated legislation (regulations etc.) and in courts (the third branch of government) the judiciary also have a "law-making function" in developing the common law, being the historical collection of the decisions of courts in relation to legal doctrines and the protection of rights.

The executive and legislative branches of government overlap in that ministers in the cabinet are drawn from the House of Commons and the Senate. Membership in two branches of the governmental process should not obscure the fact that the two branches' functions remain separate from both an operational point of view and for purposes of constitutional analysis.

The system is sustained by periodic general elections, which in Canada must be held at least every five years. But the question of confidence and the capacity of a prime minister and his cabinet to retain office during their five-year mandate rests with Parliament. If Parliament defeats a government by a vote of non-confidence on a major policy issue or a money bill, then there is recourse only to the appointment of a new cabinet that can command the confidence of the elected assembly, or more usually to the dissolution of the assembly and the creation of a new public mandate through an election. Although the conventional term of any Parliament can be foreshortened by a defeat in the House, its actual life is usually determined by the prime minister's power to obtain dissolution at any time he wishes to seek a renewed mandate from the electorate.

2. Ministerial Responsibility

Ministerial responsibility is the constitutional doctrine that ministers are responsible both individually and collectively to Parliament for the conduct of government. In its purest form, the doctrine holds that each minister is responsible for *everything* that occurs in his department. Public servants are held to be merely ministerial advisers, not decision-makers. The view that public servants must be anonymous and politically neutral and their work confidential is derived from this doctrine.

The concept of collective responsibility imposes an obligation on *all* ministers to support *all* of the government's policies in their public statements. If a minister cannot lend such support, he is expected to resign. This ministerial responsibility (the obligation to support all government policies or resign as a member of the cabinet) should not be confused with party solidarity (the political discipline imposed upon all members of the governing political party by the party whip).

3. Public Service Accountability and Neutrality
The doctrines of public service accountability and neutrality rest on the following precepts:

- A fundamental separation exists between politics and policy, and administration: politicians make policy decisions; public servants merely execute these decisions.
- Public servants are appointed and promoted on the basis of individual merit rather than on the basis of their political affiliation or party contribution.
- Public servants do not engage in partisan political activities.
- Public servants provide forthright and objective advice to their political superiors in private and in confidence. In return, their anonymity is protected by the ministers who publicly accept responsibility for departmental activities.
- Public servants execute policy decisions loyally and zealously, irrespective of their personal opinions or the philosophy and program of the party in power. In consideration thereof, public servants enjoy security of tenure in return for good behaviour and satisfactory performance.[1]

4. The Independence of the Judiciary Under the Rule of Law
The underlying concept of the supremacy of the rule of law is central to our democratic society. The concept of the rule of law is often expressed in simplistic terms as "government under law"

or "government of laws and not of men". The term "rule of law" is often used without defining its context but is generally understood to include:

- the right of an individual whose interests are affected by a judicial or administrative decision to seek redress of a grievance before a court or another authoritative body;
- the right to a rationally justified decision in respect of issues in dispute;
- the right to an unbiased hearing by *independent* decision-makers who decide the issues free of pressures from superiors, political powers or popular sentiment.

The adjudication and enforcement of the rule of law is the responsibility of the judiciary which must exercise its jurisdiction to ensure that governments obey and abide by the specific legislation and legal conventions that order parliamentary government. The rule of law applies to governments and private individuals alike.*

In order to be effective in this role, there must be an arms length relationship between the government and the judiciary. The traditions of an independent judiciary are deeply embedded in constitutional practice in Canada, despite the fact that our judicial systems were created by ordinary statute rather than as constitutionally entrenched institutions.

5. *The Government's Responsibility to Govern*

Under a parliamentary system, there can be no government unless all the members of the House of Commons co-operate with one another. The constitutional function of the House is not to govern, but rather *to support* a government.[2] This does not mean that the House should never defeat a government. Ordinarily, if the government is in a minority position it will be defeated as soon as the opposition parties decide that their partisan commitments require them to bring it down. Members of Parliament, nonetheless, have an obligation to act as good members of the House— that is, to put the maintenance of the constitutional system ahead of personal and party interests whenever necessary.[3]

---

*However, in Canada, under Section 16 of the *Interpretation Act*, R.S.C. 1970, Chap.I-23, no federal enactment is binding upon the Crown unless specifically stated.

6. The Right of the House of Commons
   to Withhold Financial Support

The centre of parliamentary power is, in theory, the power of the purse. This power rests on the notion that the people's representatives in Parliament have the right to withhold money supply from the executive unless the executive renders an accounting and resolves grievances lodged in Parliament. As early as the 15th century, it was established that requests by the King for money were to be dealt with first in the House of Commons, that the agreement of both Houses was necessary for a grant, and that any grant agreed upon was to be reported to the King by the Speaker of the House of Commons.[4]

7. The Right of the Government to Initiate Money Bills

Although Parliament has the right to withhold money supply, it cannot initiate money bills. Only the executive has that right. This division of responsibility rests on the historical principle that the Crown, having the duty to govern, should take the initiative in deciding how public funds are to be used; and Parliament, having the duty to represent the people, should have the power to scrutinize and, if necessary, to check this initiative.

8. The Right of Individual Members of Parliament
   to Initiate Legislation, Resolve Grievances, and
   Represent Their Constituents

Parliamentary government also embraces the principle that individual members of Parliament, democratically elected, have the right to represent their constituents through both the initiation of legislation and the pressing of grievances for resolution.

The rules of parliamentary procedure provide mechanisms to enable private members to draft and table legislative proposals. In practice however, a private member's bill rarely becomes law. There are simply too many obstacles to overcome.

The Changing Nature of
Parliamentary Government in Canada

MAJOR FACTORS CONTRIBUTING TO CHANGE

A number of factors, some universal, others more particulary Canadian, have contributed to the changing role of parliamentary government in Canada. It has been suggested that "Technological and industrial developments, population growth and mobility, and the rise of modern egalitarianism and the mass society, have between them led to a most formidable elaboration of the agendas of government . . ." in all parts of the democratic world.[5]

In a study done for the Trilateral Commission in 1975, the authors describe the problem of "government overload" in industrialized countries as being stimulated by:

• the involvement of an increasing proportion of the population in political activity;
• the development of new groups and of new consciousness on the part of old groups, including youth, regional groups, and ethnic minorities;
• the diversification of the political means and tactics which groups use to secure their ends;
• an increasing expectation on the part of groups that government has the responsibility to meet their needs; and an escalation in what they conceive those needs to be.[6]

The Canadian political system has been profoundly affected by these and other phenomena which today form an essential part of the backdrop against which most Canadians view their political experiences. Moreover the extent to which government has become "overloaded" is itself a political issue upon which opinion is significantly divided within Canadian political parties as well as among Canadians generally.

The following have been identified as the major factors which cause or are affected by the changing role of parliamentary government in Canada:

1. Public participation, communications and technology
2. Growth in the size and complexity of government
3. Extra-parliamentary activity
4. Representation in Parliament
5. Growth of prime-ministerial power
6. Growth of executive power
7. Growth of Parliament's overall effectiveness
8. Growth of executive federalism
9. The operation of political parties in Parliament.

1. Public Participation, Communications and Technology

Greater interest and participation in the political process by Canadians in all parts of the country, combined with rapid technological developments, particularly in the field of communications, have presented parliamentary government with some complex challenges. The House of Commons in Ottawa, once the undisputed central forum for debate on national affairs, no longer commands its historical position. Today, there are many forums and these, especially with the aid of television, have divided public attention. In the competition for public attention, politicians have been quick to employ new techniques and vehicles which enable them to keep in touch with their electors. Communications equipment of all kinds including television and jet aircraft now allow members of Parliament to reach out across the land to a degree that was unimaginable only two decades ago.

The implications of these developments for parliamentary government are far-reaching. Government and party leaders increasingly are focusing their attention on the electorate—where the votes are—and not on Parliament. How effectively a political leader projects through the media has become a decisive factor in the success or failure of day-to-day politics. Major political events such as first ministers' conferences are conducted before television cameras and are judged largely on the basis of their media impact.

Greater public participation in the political process and advances in communications and technology need not have negative consequences for parliamentary government. On the contrary, many parliamentarians recognize that television and advanced techniques of information organization and distribution are helping to make parliamentary government more accountable and efficient. Some members point with satisfaction to the benefits of televising the daily question period. Many maintain that televising proceedings of parliamentary committees would have a significant impact on improving political accountability and legislative performance. Some members also express interest in the application of computer technology to the operations of their individual offices, particularly in aid of their efforts to cope with the growing mass of information.

The technological revolution is having a profound effect on parliamentary government. Parliamentarians, however, are confident that the institutions of Parliament and these technological advances can be reconciled to the ultimate advantage of the parliamentary system.

2. Growth in the Size and Complexity of Government

By whatever measure one chooses to use, the growth in size and complexity of modern democratic governments is an established fact. In Canada, between 1960 and 1983, total federal government expenditures grew from $6.4 billion to over $90 billion, or by over 1000 per cent calculated in current dollars. Government now accounts for about 41 per cent of the gross national product — an increase of 10 per cent over the past two decades.

Provincial and local government expenditures have grown more rapidly than federal expenditures. Taxes have increased significantly whether expressed as a percentage of marginal income or in terms of "tax expenditures". The use of the tax system for public-policy purposes, not related directly to revenue generation, increased at an even more rapid rate in the 1970s than did direct expenditures. Examples are the tax incentives granted to stimulate multiple unit residential buildings (MURBs) and those designed to assist the domestic film industry.

The volume of government regulation, even if measured roughly by the number of pages in the *Canada Gazette*, has increased several times over. The number of government agencies, Crown corporations, departments, and ministries has also increased significantly, as has the incidence of major reorganization within government.

These quantitative indicators tell only part of the story. The development of numerous government programs, which enjoy widespread public support, was in response to real problems in the fields of health, welfare, education, culture, and economic management. Others reflect a general rise in public expectations — expectations too often based on the tacit assumption that government can and should solve all problems. Government promises and pronouncements often encourage such expectations. The result is an increasingly large and ponderous bureaucratic apparatus in which there are built-in incentives for future growth. These include: the absence of any reliable signals to consumers of public services about the real costs of government services, and hence the tendency to encourage consumption and demand as if they were free; the reward system of the public service, which is based to a large

9

extent on the number of subordinates supervised; and the rapid increase in government revenue due to earlier economic growth and the "benefit" of inflation, both of which enable government to acquire a higher proportion of its revenue without appearing to impose new taxes. These built-in, often perverse, incentives have contributed to growth for its own sake.

Clearly, government is not capable of effectively satisfying existing demands. The strength of anti-government and anti-bureaucracy sentiment at present are evidence of this. The disappointment and frustration of the public and the contradictory signals given to elected representatives raise the question of what functions can and should be left to private market mechanisms and/or to private forms of co-operative and community endeavour, and what functions belong with government?

The impact of big government on our parliamentary institutions is a subject of widespread and deep concern among many parliamentarians. The consensus is that our institutions must change significantly if the agreed upon aspects of the "overload"* factor are to be dealt with effectively.

The Honourable Robert Stanfield expressed the view that: ". . . parliamentary responsible government is not fitted for what it is being asked to do . . . both the government and Parliament are overloaded to the point that we have poor government; and Parliament cannot cope with government."[7]

3. Extra-Parliamentary Activity

Canadian society has always been dependent upon some minimum co-ordination between governmental and private decisions, particularly those made by large private institutions, corporations, labour unions, and special interest groups. Political debate over the last two decades has increasingly drawn attention to the fact that many private decisions have far-reaching effects on the public in general and on regions and groups in particular. As a consequence, numerous agencies and mechanisms have emerged to foster consultation and consensus between the public and private sectors. Most of these forums have developed without regard to their effects on Parliament. Parliament, on the other hand, has actively encouraged their creation without considering how such mechanisms, though useful in many respects, may enhance the

---

*See pages 35 and 64.

influence of the executive and the public service at the expense of Parliament.

Studies show that special interest groups pay little attention to Parliament and tend to focus their lobbying efforts on ministers and the bureaucracy. The executive, in addition to its frequent use of departmental advisory committees and consultative bodies, employs several broader consultative forums such as Royal Commissions and devices such as white papers, green papers, and task forces. These broader mechanisms have few, if any, direct links with Parliament or individual members. Permanent research bodies such as the Economic Council of Canada and the Science Council of Canada were created in the mid 1960s as advisory appendages of the executive. Little thought was given to their possible links to Parliament.

In respect of its management of the economy, the government has indicated a growing awareness of the importance of consultation. In the wake of the 1975 wage and price controls program, the government has encouraged numerous discussions concerning the possible development of broad forums for consultation on the management of the economy. A desire on the part of labour to be regarded as an equal partner with government in such a forum has proved to be unacceptable to many, however, who argue that the supremacy of government, responsible to all Canadians, must not be jeopardized by representatives of special interest groups. However, little has been heard about the real challenge such a forum would likely pose to Parliament by concentrating discussion and analysis in the executive branch of government.

Also, in April 1982, the minister of finance, Allan MacEachen, issued a Green Paper on the Budget Process calling for the establishment of consultative bodies to advise and comment on proposed budget measures. Subsequently, his successor, Marc Lalonde, appointed a committee of academic advisers to provide advice on a continuing basis. Again, the reality is that public policy formulation and decision-making are carried on remote from Parliament in a forum established and controlled by the executive.

While recognizing that the activities of special interest groups and public policy advisory bodies are legitimate and desirable, there remains a widespread concern that Parliament does not ordinarily have a satisfactory role to play in the formulation of public policy. Many parliamentarians in the House of Commons and the

Senate share the view that virtually all important public policy issues should be discussed in Parliament, and that the executive should ensure that this happens. This view is legitimate. It is certainly within the capacity of the executive to refer many more matters to Parliament for discussion.

4. Representation in Parliament

The Canadian political system has always been strained in terms of ensuring equitable representation from among the diverse interests, groups, and regions across Canada. Recently however, concern about the "representativeness" of Parliament has reached new heights.

The single-member-constituency, simple-plurality system for electing members of Parliament has frequently produced a House of Commons with a membership bearing little relationship to the popular vote achieved regionally by the main political parties. In the past this has resulted in a significant "underrepresentation" of the Progressive Conservative Party strength in Quebec and a corresponding weakness of the Liberal Party in the prairie provinces. This strongly suggests that the democratic base of Canadian parliamentary government could be strengthened by a modified system, which would better reflect the regional distribution of political support while continuing to ensure a reasonable likelihood of producing a majority government. The Task Force on Canadian Unity focussed on this problem and recommended that 60 new members of Parliament be elected from provincial lists according to party vote.

Concern about the representativeness of Parliament has also been noted in recent proposals for Senate reform.* It is generally perceived that the Senate (which was originally created to effect regional representation at the national level) has not satisfied the objectives of the Fathers of Confederation. The 1978 Constitutional Amendment Bill proposed ways to improve regional representation in national debate by giving provincial governments power of appointment for half of the Senate seats.

In 1981, the Prime Minister suggested that he would favour a serious review of these questions with a view to securing stronger regional representation in Parliament and other national institutions such as the Supreme Court of Canada and powerful tribunals

---

*See later in this study page 101.

such as the Canadian Radio-television and Telecommunications Commission. We strongly endorse the need for such a review but we are concerned that an issue such as proportional representation may be separated from, or will be offered as a substitute for, other essential reforms of parliamentary government. For example, we question whether there is much to be gained by increased regional representation through a system of proportional representation if the House of Commons continues to impose strict adherence to party discipline and enforces rigid rules of want of confidence, thereby making it extremely difficult for such voices to be heard once they are elected.

Parliamentary reform must be considered in close relation to the electoral basis of representation itself.

The issue of *parliamentary representation* is not addressed in any detail in this study. It is a complex and sensitive subject requiring careful study and analysis. The authors share the opinion of most parliamentarians, however, that parliamentary representation should be a central consideration in any comprehensive program for institutional reform.

Some of the alternatives currently being proposed for Senate reform are presented later in this study to provide the reader with some appreciation of the wide range of possibilities that have been suggested and their likely impact on parliamentary operations and the legislative process.

5. Growth of Prime Ministerial Power

The prime minister has always been first among equals in his relations with his cabinet colleagues. However, he has no equal in relation to Parliament; in this respect, he is the single most powerful individual politician in Parliament.

The formal powers of the prime minister are extensive, and include the following:

• dissolution and convocation, of Parliament;
• appointment and dismissal of cabinet ministers, deputy ministers, and the heads of numerous government agencies, regulatory bodies, and crown corporations;
• appointment of chief justices of all courts;
• control of the agenda and deliberations of cabinet.

In addition, the prime minister enjoys great political influence as

13

a result of his positions as leader of the government, leader of the majority political party, spokesman for the activities and policies of government as a whole, and the member of government most visible to the Canadian public. Because of these powers and prerogatives, the prime minister commands a degree of authority unavailable to other ministers, let alone ordinary members of Parliament.

During the last two decades, the power of the prime minister has grown for several reasons. First, there is greater "grassroots" involvement in political parties now than was formerly the case and the prime minister is elected in this broadly-based democratically-run forum. The result is that the prime minister achieves greater authority among his political colleagues. Second, the conduct of political party conventions and elections in the age of television and instant communications draws special attention to the leader, and the prime minister has the easiest access to the media. Third, the prime minister, especially since 1968, has significantly improved the resources and capabilities of his personal office.[8]

Prime Minister Trudeau's rationale for enlarging his office was to meet two principal objectives: to exercise a greater degree of collective political control over a large and complex government apparatus and to respond more effectively to the increased demands upon Parliament, government and himself by a more active and interested public.[9] The practical effect of Prime Minister Trudeau's actions was to increase his dominance over Parliament, the cabinet and the public service.

This growth in prime ministerial power and its impact on parliamentary government is a deep preoccupation of many parliamentarians including a number of former Liberal cabinet ministers. Few suggest that the formal powers of the prime minister should be curbed because they recognize that the prime minister must provide strong leadership. Nonetheless, most express the hope that a prudent exercise of prime ministerial prerogatives will restore balance to the relationships between the prime minister and Parliament.

It is essential, however, to keep prime ministerial power in perspective. The prime minister can be constrained by the collective will of his cabinet colleagues, by his parliamentary party caucus, and to a degree by the Opposition. Responsibility for the effective use of such instruments to enforce a satisfactory degree of accountability remains in the hands of parliamentarians on both sides of the House.

6. *Growth of Executive Power*

The cabinet has always exercised great influence in relation to Parliament. Recently, however, its importance has been considerably increased by developments related to the executive branch and the bureaucracy of government.

First, much of the legislation passed by Parliament has tended increasingly to confer more and more discretionary authority on the cabinet as a whole, on individual ministers, and on senior public servants.

Second, in considering the growth and influence of executive power, the role of the central agencies deserves mention. Central agencies are charged with coordinating and monitoring government activities and policies and with developing certain key policies for government. Unlike traditional "line" departments, central agencies have responsibilities which "are crucial to the *common* interests of government departments and which relate to matters of major importance."[10] At the federal level, the major central agencies are the following:

- the privy council office (PCO), which services the cabinet and undertakes strategic planning and policy analysis for the government as a whole;
- the prime minister's office (PMO), which assists the prime minister in the performance of his manifold functions and also provides him with timely political and policy advice;
- the department of finance, which is statutorily charged with developing the government's fiscal, taxation and economic policies and with monitoring domestic and international economic conditions;
- the treasury board secretariat, which is charged with the control of government expenditures and the management of its human resources; it operates under the treasury board, a cabinet committee that is formally responsible for these activities.

Other central agencies include the newly created comptroller general's office, the ministry of state for economic and regional development, and the ministry of state for social development.

These agencies have been significantly strengthened and enlarged in recent years, and they are staffed by highly qualified

15

specialists. They provide the government with an improved capacity to control and direct what its hundreds of thousands of public servants and dozens of departments do.

Third, the executive as a whole has greatly increased the volume and sophistication of its statistical data and other information gathering activities along with its capacity to analyse and utilize such information. In effect, a "policy analysis industry" now exists within the framework of the executive branch of government.

These developments are protected by the continued existence of strong legal and bureaucratic norms and practices which favour government secrecy and an excessive proprietary claim on information of all kinds. Those interviewed in connection with this study were virtually unanimous in their criticism of executive and governmental secrecy and in their advocacy of strong freedom of information laws.* Most parliamentarians agree that effective government requires a strong executive, supported by an efficient and competent public service. There is, however, continuing concern about the relative inability of Parliament to hold the executive to account. Cause for alarm is derived not only from the weakness of the mechanisms to achieve executive accountability, but also the attitudes of those occupying the government front benches. These attitudes are still described by many as "uncooperative", "secretive", "unforthcoming", "elitist" and "condescending".

Clearly, achieving a balanced and co-operative relationship between the executive and Parliament must be regarded as an essential objective of parliamentary government if the institutions of Parliament are to function effectively.

7. Growth of Parliament's Overall Effectiveness

Although prime ministerial and executive power has increased substantially over the past decade, Parliament, too, has made important advances in terms of its effectiveness. Organizational and procedural changes have contributed to an increase in the overall effectiveness of Parliament. The Honourable John Reid recalls:

> "I first came to Ottawa in 1963 as an assistant to a minister. I was elected to the House two years later. In those days, two members shared an office, with one telephone. They had one secretary . . .

---

*Parliamentarians acted on this concern by passing the *Access to Information Act*, S.C., 1980-81-82, Chap. 111.

"In those days members had to pay for their long distance telephone calls. They had no weekly air ticket or free passes home as they have today. The Library of Parliament had not yet begun to develop a research facility, and there was no money for caucus research, and no money for leaders' research staff . . .

"Today most members have a two-room office in Ottawa staffed by three aides. Under new regulations that recently came down from the committee on members' services and approved by the Committee of Internal Economy, members can now hire research staff. And members now have control over their staff in terms of what functions they will perform. Members now have a fixed budget . . .

"The Library provides, in my judgment, very good to excellent research material. The caucus research offices provide very good material from a partisan point of view. It we add to this, vastly improved transportation, communication and constituency facilities . . . there is little excuse for members attending meetings unprepared."[11]

Mr. Reid's remarks also drew attention to improvements in the organization and function of the parliamentary committee system and to improvements in the operations of the House that have been brought about by the ability of the Standing Committee on Public Accounts to define the scope of its activities at the beginning of the session. He also noted the creation of the Joint Committee on Regulations and Other Statutory Instruments whose role is to scrutinize the exercise of delegated legislative authority, and the introduction of radio and television broadcasting of parliamentary proceedings.

On May 31, 1982 a House of Commons Special Committee on Standing Orders and Procedure was struck to study House procedures and to make recommendations directed at improving parliamentary procedure. In its Third Report, the Committee noted:

"The reform of parliamentary procedure should be an ongoing process. Parliament is in a constant state of evolution, and if its practices are to be effective, they must be adapted when necessary to meet the changing needs of Parliament and reflect the changing conditions of society and the nation."[12]

The Committee subsequently recommended substantive procedural changes which were adopted by the House on a one-year provisional basis on November 29, 1982.

However, the essential problems centering on accountability and legislative performance remain unresolved. The root cause is the continuing imbalance between parliamentary power and prime ministerial and executive power.

8. Growth of Executive Federalism

The reality of Canadian federalism is nowhere more evident than in the proliferation of federal-provincial committees and meetings at both the ministerial and official levels. The development of this "executive federalism" is due to many of the factors and incentives already examined. It also reflects the numerous joint expenditure programs, tax and fiscal agreements, and regulatory and administrative dependencies created by overlapping jurisdictions and the increased professionalism of the provinces' public services.

It is sometimes said that the real opposition to the federal government comes not from the opposition parties, but from the provincial governments who collectively possess substantial countervailing power. It is important to note, however, that the provincial legislatures are left out of the federal-provincial/executive struggle as much as the federal Parliament. The central problem, therefore, is that decisions reached in the federal-provincial arenas are, in a real sense, beyond the reach of any meaningful scrutiny by Parliament.

Canadian parliamentarians as well as many other informed observers of Canadian government, express deep concern about the degree to which executive federalism is circumventing parliamentary and legislative channels. Professor Donald Smiley, a noted authority on Canadian federalism, writes:

> "The lack of parliamentary involvement in federal-provincial relations is demonstrated not only in situations where it is restricted to the *post hoc* ratification of actions already agreed upon by the two levels of government, but also by governments by-passing their respective legislatures in announcing future policies."[13]

It seems necessary to accept that continuing direct interaction between federal ministers and officials and their provincial counterparts is inevitable. A more active role for Parliament and the legislatures in the process could be developed if federal and provincial government leaders were to change their attitudes and refer more matters for discussion and debate to their respective legislatures.

9. The Operation of Political Parties in Parliament

Outside Parliament, political parties in Canada have generally become more democratic, particularly in terms of electing leaders and devising platforms. Within the parliamentary system, however, political parties apply the whips when it comes to major dissent at the time of voting and when divisions on the vote occur. Despite periodic free votes on issues like capital punishment, opportunities for individual independence are limited both in the House as a whole and in the operation of its committees.

More formal consultation now occurs between the leadership of the parties in Parliament and their caucuses through weekly *in camera* meetings. However, these sessions, too, are constrained by discipline and by lack of time and information. Backbench members in the government party who aspire to future promotion to the cabinet learn quickly that their compliance with party discipline is absolutely essential.

Although most parliamentarians recognize that party discipline is essential for effective governing, many of them nonetheless express their deep dissatisfaction with those conventions of party discipline that stifle individual initiative. They argue that a middle ground exists and that relations between front bench and back bench members would improve and become more productive if attitudes and the rules relating to confidence were relaxed.

THE IMPACT OF CHANGE

The foregoing outline of the traditional principles of parliamentary government, considered in relation to the changing nature of parliamentary government in Canada, should leave no doubt that practice today varies significantly from theory.

The prime minister, traditionally "first among equals", now dominates both the cabinet and Parliament. Even former cabinet ministers readily attest that real collective decision-making in cabinet has diminished as the influence of the prime minister has increased. In real terms, the influence of the prime minister in Canada's parliamentary system is overwhelming.

General elections have largely become competitions between the party leaders for the prime minister's office. We concentrate our attention upon the leaders and the parties encourage us to do so. Once in office we observe the prime minister exercising almost tyrannical power over his ministers and backbenchers. It is not unusual for a prime minister to ignore the House of Commons entirely or treat it with disdain, unless he perceives that the public is watching. Our most recent prime ministers have admitted their predominance over the House of Commons and argued the need for this power.[14]

The prime minister's power notwithstanding, the power of ministers, both individual and collective, has increased rapidly in relation to Parliament.

Finally, the public service operates increasingly beyond the direct control of ministers to whom, in theory, it is accountable.

In the face of these developments, *Parliament is no longer able to exact effective accountability from the prime minister and the executive* for policy and administration or for public expenditure. Members of Parliament, whether as individuals, members of committees, or in opposition, have lost ground in two important respects: in holding the executive to account and in shaping legislation.

Does this matter?

On the one hand, there is little point in lamenting the changes in society—human, environmental and technological—that have contributed to a larger, more complex and sophisticated government. Parliamentary government in Canada had to evolve with the times. The business of government has to be carried on efficiently— irrespective of its changing environment and its increasing burden. Noting the importance of the government's responsibility to govern and get on with the job, some frontbenchers still complain that the Opposition is uncooperative and obstreperous and is not sufficiently aware of the fundamental nature of the government's responsibility. They point to the rapid growth in prime ministerial and executive power as a form of natural evolution in response to the need for stronger leadership and more effective co-ordination of policies.

On the other hand, the business of government is like no other. Government makes the rules by which we must abide. We have no choice but to obey them. It extracts from us and spends huge sums of money. Its policies influence virtually every aspect of our daily lives and our expectations for the future. Clearly, the grant of such awesome power by the people to its government is made only on the condition that the government remain accountable on a continuing basis for the exercise of that power. Parliament was conceived and intended to be the principal vehicle to exact that accountability during the period between elections.

The demands of efficiency will always war with the demands of accountability. A process of policy formulation which allows for effective scrutiny by Parliament is bound to be time-consuming and often frustrating.* The danger is that events may pass us by, that circumstances may get out of control if decision-making is unduly delayed or inconsistent.

So, yes, it does matter if, in the pursuit of efficiency, Parliament is seriously weakened. In the following sections we explore how to strike a new balance between efficiency and accountability.

---

*The advantage of detailed committee study is that legislation that follows committee recommendations may move speedily through the House.

PARLIAMENTARY GOVERNMENT AT THE CROSSROADS: MAJOR ISSUES FOR REFORM

The Accountability of the Executive and of the Public Service to Parliament for Policy and Administration

ACCOUNTABILITY IN THEORY AND PRACTICE

Canadian parliamentary government is based on a system of accountability that requires the cabinet and the public service to render an accounting to Parliament through the executive. The accountability of the cabinet is direct; the accountability of the public service is indirect.

The system is intended to secure fundamental accountability — that is, to hold a clearly identifiable group of elected politicians responsible for the ways, and ends to which, the coercive power of the state is applied.

The effective operation of this system of accountability depends upon a subtle interplay among three elements: individual ministerial responsibility; the collective responsibility of the cabinet; and the anonymity and neutrality of the public service.[15]

A study undertaken for the Australian Government contends that for such interplay to succeed, several conditions must be met. The allocation of responsibilities among departments must be precisely enough defined so that each minister can be held responsible for a clearly delineated policy area and there is no ambiguity which may allow responsibility to be evaded. Policy instructions from a minister or cabinet must also be sufficiently precise to ensure that departmental officers have a clear idea of what a minister's will is on a given matter. A minister must be prepared to shield his officers from public criticism. Finally, a clearly understood division of responsibilities must exist between a minister and the permanent head (the deputy minister) of a department so that the continuity of administration is not disturbed by conflict over jurisdiction.[16]

In practice, in Canada and elsewhere, these conditions are *not* met and it is generally recognized that "at present, Parliament does not exercise effective power, in the sense of control and influence, over the executive in general and the public service in particular."[17]

INDIVIDUAL AND COLLECTIVE MINISTERIAL RESPONSIBILITY

The descrepancies between the theory and practice of ministerial responsibility are most apparent when viewed against the total obligations discharged by an individual minister. Although a minister is theoretically responsible for *all* the policies and activities of his department, this constitutes a practical impossibility. The scope of governmental activity is simply too wide; it is often technically complex; many departments are enormous and include satellite agencies with varying degrees of independence; and ministers cannot make important personnel and financial decisions on their own.

The concept of individual ministerial responsibility is seriously strained when applied to Canadian parliamentary government. Part of the problem stems from the inconsistent way in which parliamentarians on both sides of the House interpret ministerial responsibility to their own partisan advantage. Opposition members continually accuse the cabinet as well as individual ministers of applying varying interpretations of convention for purposes of administrative convenience and evading responsibility for maladministration.[18] In fact, ministers have tended to be restrictive in their interpretation of the convention that requires a minister to resign if a serious error committed by his department is exposed. The contrast between Canadian and British practice in this connection was dramatically demonstrated in the spring of 1982 when the British Foreign Secretary resigned immediately upon the Argentine invasion of the Falkland Islands.

Although there is inconsistency between the theory and practice of individual ministerial responsibility, this does not mean that the convention is totally disregarded or without value. The convention is enforced partially through the functioning of Parliament as a forum in which ministers must answer questions and respond to criticisms of their departments. Ministers are also forcibly reminded of their responsibility for all aspects of their departments when they face the media and contend with the pressures and conflicts associated with intergovernmental relations. The gap between theory and practice is wide, however, and scepticism increases in the face of such practices of the recent past as:

• the establishment (albeit briefly) of a rotating roster of ministers required to be present in Parliament during question period — thus reducing the opportunity for the Opposition to question specific ministers on any given day;
• the shifting of ministerial portfolios with such frequency that some departments had a new minister virtually every year; and
• the Speaker's ruling that ministers do not have to answer questions on matters relating to former portfolios.

Ministerial responsibility should not be confused with the cut and thrust of parliamentary debate known as "parliamentary answerability". Although debate is a visible part of it, the most important aspects of responsibility are those which create a system of control over the public service.

While individual ministerial responsibility in Canada seems to be as honoured in the breach as in the observance, collective ministerial responsibility remains an important operating concept. Many former cabinet ministers agree that the collective basis for decision-making has improved significantly through the expanded use of cabinet committees. Cabinet committees have also made it easier for ministers to co-ordinate departmental policy and administration. This is especially the case under the cabinet "envelope" system adopted in 1979 by the Clark government. Ministers also appreciate that in order for cabinet to maintain the confidence of the House of Commons all members of cabinet must support government policy in their public utterances.

ACCOUNTABILITY IN OTHER COUNTRIES

Discrepancies between the theory and practice of executive and public service accountability to Parliament also exist in other countries with parliamentary systems of government. In the United Kingdom, the 1978 Select Committee on Procedure of the House of Commons concluded that:

"The balance of advantage between Parliament and the government in the day to day working of the Constitution is now weighted in favour of the government to a degree which arouses widespread anxiety and is inimical to the proper working of our parliamentary democracy."[19]

A comparative analysis of accountability in the United Kingdom and Australia prepared for the Coombes Commission in Australia also considers the difficulties of applying the principle of ministerial responsibility in practice. The study concludes that:

"... individual ministerial responsibility has acquired a more limited and particular significance in the modern state. As a doctrine of answerability it continues to provide Parliament with a basic method of scrutinizing the administration. By holding ministers answerable to Parliament, and by establishing a residual capacity to punish ministers for purely personal transgressions, the doctrine still contributes significantly to the particular meaning of responsible government. However, as a doctrine of political control its effective reality is in question, because it is difficult to say that, by itself, the concept provides any clear rule as to how far and in what circumstances a minister can be held accountable, in any positive sense, for the detailed administrative activities with which he is associated."[20]

Clearly, the problems of executive and public service accountability are not uniquely Canadian.

Changes that strengthen the role of Parliament will assist in effecting greater political control over the public service.* The intricacy and subtlety of the central elements of the accountability system—individual and collective ministerial responsibility—must not be under-rated because it is within the framework of these basic elements of accountability in parliamentary government that the more particular mechanisms of accountability operate.

MECHANISMS OF ACCOUNTABILITY

Parliamentary mechanisms to secure executive accountability include:

• general debate
• questions to ministers
• standing committees (to review spending estimates and legislation)
• ad hoc and special committees

---

*We do not deal here with the intricacies of internal public service management—an area fully examined in 1977 by the Royal Commission on Financial Management and Accountability (The Lambert Commission).

• special agencies, which report to Parliament (such as the Auditor General's office, the Commissioner of Official Languages, the Public Service Commission, and the Human Rights Commission).

These mechanisms are potentially effective bases for scrutiny. Each mechanism, however, has weaknesses.

General parliamentary debate on new legislation, tax measures, and topics selected by the Opposition on opposition days is still, in terms of parliamentary time, the principal mechanism of accountability. Such debate is generally effective in identifying the main controversies and alternatives related to particular items of legislation for public scrutiny and education. However, other than the speech from the throne (which is usually perfunctory), and the publication of the five-year expenditure plan that accompanies the budget speech, there is little requirement for the government or the Opposition to explain, justify or debate its priorities, for either the forthcoming year or the medium-term future. Moreover, debates on particular bills tend to be long and repetitive. Rigid parliamentary procedures elevate the "general principle" stage in the passage of legislation to the point where there is little time for detailed scrutiny.[21]

Questions to ministers during the daily question period and in the context of debate on bills are the most visible test of ministerial and Opposition mettle. At the same time, however, it is acknowledged by most experienced parliamentarians that question period is not suited to detailed follow-up and scrutiny, except perhaps by the continued wearing down of a minister over a period of days and weeks.

Parliamentary committees should provide an additional means of holding ministers accountable. Unfortunately, ministers do not, as a rule, devote much time to committee work and cannot be compelled to attend committee meetings.

Special agencies including the Auditor General's office, the Commissioner of Official Languages, the Human Rights Commission, and the Public Service Commission further the process of parliamentary scrutiny. The Auditor General's office, for example, prepares the audit of the public accounts and the Auditor General's report forms the basis of much of the activity of the

Public Accounts Committee (one of two committees chaired by a member of the Opposition). In recent years the Auditor General has also conducted and published comprehensive "value for money" audits of individual departments. The Commissioner of Official languages, as another example, scrutinizes on behalf of Parliament the implementation of the *Official Languages Act.*

The visibility and success of these offices has been due in part to the fact that their reports are often refreshingly readable, frank and blunt in their criticisms. However, questions of accountability can be applied as forcefully to these agencies as to the departments they scrutinize. Many parliamentarians and public servants are very critical of the degree to which the Auditor General's concept of "value for money" has served as a basis for his passing judgment on policy matters rather than financial practices. They are also concerned that this concept will lead to an evaluation of programs on narrow financial grounds. More importantly, however, there is serious concern that the role of the Auditor General should not usurp the function of Parliament to evaluate programs and criticize policy. We share these concerns and we urge that the Auditor General's powers be reviewed to ensure that they do not diminish Parliament's role in criticizing policy and evaluating programs.

At present, specialized agencies of Parliament do not report to any single authority. In some cases they are responsible to the Speaker of the House. In others, nominal control is the responsibility of a committee. In all cases, however, the treasury board exerts considerable influence over the resources allocated to these agencies. Clearly, if future reform involves the establishment of new agencies that are attached directly to Parliament, then their roles and reporting relationships will have to be clarified.

The amended House Rules that were adopted on a one-year provisional basis on November 29, 1982 will be of some assistance here in that annual reports tabled by departments, Crown corporations and other agencies reporting to Parliament, will be referred automatically to a standing committee as designated by the member tabling the report. A tradition of review and accountability in committee will no doubt grow as the committees begin to exploit their new powers and jurisdiction.

THE QUESTION OF WANT OF CONFIDENCE AND POLITICAL PARTY DISCIPLINE
Any reform that is likely to exact greater accountability of the

executive to Parliament begs the question of whether every vote in the House of Commons should be considered to be a vote of confidence. The executive cannot govern without the confidence of the House, but individual members of Parliament are not permitted to express their independent views in debate or with their votes; an individual member's disagreement with the executive's position is therefore tantamount to a threat to bring down the government. Thus, a paradox emerges when the confidence issue is examined.

On the one hand, successive governments seem compelled, publicly, to treat every issue as one of confidence; defeat cannot be tolerated. On the other hand, members of Parliament of virtually all political persuasions agree that governments can and should accept amendments, and even defeats, on some matters. In the final analysis, nearly everyone agrees that confidence is what the government says it is and the government decides on which issues it will resign or seek dissolution of the House. However, even with this pragmatic approach to the question of confidence, governments and parties continue to exercise rigid party discipline. Consequently, members of Parliament are expressing growing concern over their inability to act independently.

Most members of Parliament have already expressed their willingness to support measures that would relax the rules with respect to confidence and allow greater freedom for individual and cross-party voting. They welcome the idea of more free votes in the House and more frequent acceptance of legislative amendments by the cabinet. These developments would also create opportunities and incentives for parliamentary committees to become political forums which members of Parliament would take more seriously.

Some parliamentarians support the idea of formal codification of a set of simple straightforward rules of confidence. Confidence would continue to apply to the throne speech, the budget, the estimates in total, and to issues that the government views, and announces, as issues of confidence. No one regards the codification of rules as a panacea, nor does anyone underestimate the initial difficulty that might be involved in adjusting to such changes. Other members of Parliament support the idea of confidence evolving along the lines described but they do not support the notion of formal codification.

Only a tiny minority express little enthusiasm for any change in the rules of confidence. Of these, a few argue that it would lead to a congressional system of government. Others maintain that any relaxation of the rules would weaken the capacity of the government to take strong and sometimes unpopular decisions in the national interest. In contrast, those who favour the loosening of the rules of confidence and eliminating the tyranny of the party whips argue that this will better serve the national interest by allowing Parliament, through the more independent action of its members, to reflect the interests of Canadians more properly. We recommend that:

1. **The leaders of both the government and opposition parties recognize and adopt in practice a less stringent approach to the question of party discipline and the rules governing confidence.**

We have stopped short of recommending the codification of the rules of confidence because we consider such a step to be unnecessary.

POLITICAL PARTIES IN PARLIAMENT:
CAUCUS, FRONTBENCHERS AND BACKBENCHERS

Some government members contend that many of the significant advances in holding the executive to account have occurred through the vehicle of regular caucus meetings. Members maintain that in this private venue, criticism and discussion are constructive and that their contributions are substantial, particularly when compared with their public roles in the activities of Parliament. Others point to the now regular meetings of the "political cabinet"— party officials and cabinet—as another improvement of the past decade.[22] Members in the major opposition parties also claim that caucus organization is better than it was, and this greater coherence has resulted in improved accountability in some legislative areas and during question period.

Despite these improvements, members of Parliament are genuinely frustrated by their inability to take independent positions and to vote accordingly because of excessive party discipline. This is especially the case on regional issues where views within political parties differ significantly. It is not surprising, therefore, that many members resent the fact that their provincial governments are more readily viewed as legitimate spokesmen for regional interests than they are.

It should also come as no surprise that views about loosening the reins of party discipline vary according to whether a member is a frontbencher or a backbencher. Frontbenchers, generally, resist independence among their backbench colleagues simply because it makes life less complicated for them. Conversely, backbenchers, most of whom are striving for recognition and political advancement, resent their roles of hard-working, obedient puppets. The consequent tensions between front and backbenchers are part of the parliamentary dynamic and are not altogether unhealthy. However, a comment by one backbencher illustrates the frustration and impotence felt by many of his colleagues: "The frontbenchers consider us a nuisance. We are there to vote but to do little else, except, of course, to look after our constituents." The high turnover of junior members when general elections are called is in part caused by such frustrations.

We recognize the importance of party discipline in Parliament, but we have concluded, nonetheless, that along with other structural and informal changes, some loosening of the discipline now exacted by political parties on both sides of the House is required. If party discipline is not relaxed, Parliament will gradually cease to be the central forum for the expression of the legitimate interests and concerns of Canadians and will no longer serve as an effective instrument of accountability to the electorate.

Guided by the views of citizens and parliamentarians alike, we have further concluded that concrete ways must be found to allow consensus and conflict to cross party lines occasionally. Recommendations relating to the committee system discussed later in this text are pertinent here. But in addition to making the existing committee structure more efficient, we believe that members of Parliament should be free to stimulate and bring about new committee activity. At present, the rules do not specifically permit even a standing committee to begin hearings on some public issues within the broad subject area covered by the committee. (It may be possible under the November, 1982 provisional rules to initiate study in a given area by raising the issue during committee study of an annual report referred to the committee.) To allow individual members and groups of members to initiate investigations and deal with issues of national concern as they see them, we recommend that:

2. Where a minimum of 50 members of Parliament (at least ten of whom are drawn from each of two political parties) agree that a subject warrants committee investigation, a committee for such a purpose shall be created, or an existing committee shall be assigned to investigate the subject. Only two such _new_ committees should co-exist at any time during any session of Parliament.
3. Standing committees be given the power to select subjects within their jurisdiction for investigation.

The Role of the Opposition: Tactics, Information and Accountability

COMPETING TACTICS

Views concerning the legitimate role of the Opposition vary from those of non-cooperation (expressed in such terms as: "let the government die by its own mistakes" and "opposition for the sake of opposition") to more positive notions of constructive opposition (some of which elevate the opposition to the level of "alternative government" or the "government in waiting"). These divergent, tactically oriented views of the Opposition's role obviously affect the kind of accountability that can be secured from the government.

Although their behaviour is broadly conditioned by the rules and incentives of parliamentary government, the opposition parties have considerable latitude to conduct themselves as they wish; they make their own choices. Hence, the opposition parties bear a major responsibility for the nature of accountability exacted in Parliament. For example, the failure of the opposition parties to scrutinize expenditures effectively, though partly caused by the inherent weakness of the committee system, is also due to the opposition parties' assignment and rotation of committee members, and their adoption of tactics designed intentionally to attract media attention and embarrass the government. The opposition parties could if they wished, involve themselves in a more thorough scrutiny of programs.

Twenty-five days in each annual session—known as opposition days—provide members of the Opposition with an opportunity to criticize government policy and draw shortcomings in the administration of policies and programs to public attention. On allotted days, a wide variety of topics can be introduced for debate. In a recent session of Parliament, for example, the following were among topics chosen by the Opposition:

- Canada's capacity to export grain
- the establishment of a special committee to recommend changes to the Official Secrets Act
- inflation and unemployment
- Canadian control of the development of natural resources
- freedom of information
- the autopact
- lack of a competitive air transport policy
- parliamentary control of public expenditures
- guidelines respecting the use of social insurance numbers and alleged federal infringements on provincial jurisdiction

While the range of topics is considerable, it is generally agreed by parliamentarians that opposition days are not used as effectively as they might be. Two major criticisms allege lack of interest on the part of the government and the media and lack of sufficient preparation on the part of opposition spokesmen. One opposition spokesman stated:

> "Opposition days give us superb opportunities to draw public atten-
> tion to the government's faults. However, we often miss our opportunity
> because tactics get in the way . . . We try to embarrass the government
> and often our efforts backfire . . . The worst situation is to be ignored
> by both the government and the media."

While conceding that opposition parties carry a heavy responsibility for ensuring accountability, most parliamentarians agree that there is little likelihood of improvement at present, considering the highly partisan atmosphere in the House. They contend that fundamental changes in the rules of parliamentary practice— particularly the rules governing committees and confidence—will have to be made before opposition parties will adopt more serious and constructive attitudes with respect to holding the executive to account in Parliament.

OBTAINING AND USING INFORMATION
Virtually everyone agrees that modern accountability requires, at the very least, access to accurate information, honest answers to questions and the ability to understand and utilize such informa-

tion. This, then, is a joint responsibility of the government and the parties in opposition.

Recent experience indicates that the executive has the strongest vested interest in official secrecy, and that general expressions in support of greater freedom of information made by successive governments are inadequate. We have for some time been convinced that freedom of information is one reform that required a formal legislative basis. In 1979 we recommended that a freedom of information statute be enacted to ensure that relevant information and reports, acquired at public expense, are made public, subject to provisions for national security, the protection of individual privacy, and with *limited spheres* for tendering confidential advice to ministers.[23]

The passage of the *Access to Information Act* in 1982 was an important first step towards reform. We have serious reservations, however, concerning some aspects of the statute. The grounds for exemption in respect of ministerial confidentiality are not "limited spheres"—they are left undefined. Also, exceptions from the act are far too broad and numerous. As experience with the legislation is gained, we expect that stricter grounds for exemption will be required.

Viewed by the Opposition, this new legislation is a positive development but it has, in part, been offset by a serious negative development in respect of the government information process— the increased use by the government of "advocacy advertising". Unquestionably, the government has a duty as well as a right to inform citizens about programs that affect them. There is a difference, however, between information and partisan propaganda—a difference that has been ignored with increasing frequency in recent years. Canadian taxpayers should not pay for the promotion of party propaganda. However, the practice has developed to the point where, in terms of dollar volume, the federal government is now the leading advertiser in Canada. In the United States, the federal government ranks tenth.

Similar problems exist with public opinion polls commissioned by the government and paid for by taxpayers. Numerous polls have been conducted by the federal government on such diverse topics as separatism and unemployment insurance. Opinion polls *per se* have proved to be strikingly unreliable as guides for policy-making. If one is conducted, therefore, it should be standard practice to make it public immediately. This practice in itself would tend to discipline the use of them.

In fairness it must be mentioned that the increased use of advocacy advertising and opinion polls by the government is not an isolated phenomenon. Private interests and political parties in opposition (especially when their provincial confreres are in power at the provincial level) also play the information-propaganda game. In part, these activities are in response to a growing mistrust of the mass media. They also point up, however, the subtle interconnections between public and private sector institutions in the broader process of accountability.

It is important to acknowledge that there are differing opinions as to how much, and what kinds of information are needed to ensure accountability. A few argue that in no respect will easier access to information lead to more effective scrutiny of the government and its operations, so they downplay the importance of the issue. The majority view, however, is that major improvements in access to information are essential even though these may contribute to "information overload". Of course, this points up an important secondary need for equipment and resources to filter and digest information.

We contend that improved access to information will not be effectively exploited unless reforms in this connection are accompanied by other changes in party discipline, the rules of confidence, and the powers of committees.

DIRECT PUBLIC SERVICE INTERACTION WITH OPPOSITION PARTIES AND INDIVIDUAL MEMBERS OF PARLIAMENT

In theory, the public service is accountable to Parliament only indirectly through the executive. In practice, however, there are other, more direct forms of accountability.

First, public servants are increasingly called upon to appear before parliamentary committees to explain and defend administrative and, often, policy-related issues. Second, opposition party caucuses are briefed by public servants from time to time to clarify or explain a report or piece of legislation. Third, individual members have direct contact with public servants through personal friendship and mutual professional interests as well as through concerns and grievances registered by their constituents.

Such forms of direct contact raise questions about the nature of the obligations of public servants to Parliament and to the citizens of Canada as opposed to the government of the day and particular ministers. Distinctions between policy (for which public servants are not responsible) and administration (for which they are) can become difficult to maintain. For example, briefings, for opposition parties are sometimes uncomfortable affairs because party spokesmen often ask questions that touch upon policy and public servants must therefore strain—and so appear evasive or uncooperative—to avoid answering. Public servants having to deal with telephone calls or written grievances from members of Parliament on behalf of constituents may respond differently depending upon whether the member is from the government party or an opposition party, or whether the member is well known and respected or a "trouble-maker". In most instances, of course, none of these considerations arises as an issue and enquiries and grievances are resolved smoothly and expeditiously.

Our research and interviews lead us to conclude that direct contact between the public servants and individual members of Parliament in all parties should be encouraged on the general grounds that awareness of each other's role enhances understanding and should contribute to the resolution of grievances.

The Accountability of the Public Service and Ministerial/ Deputy Ministerial Relations

In the formal model of parliamentary government, the public service is accountable to the executive and the executive is, in turn, accountable to Parliament. In practice, however, the public service must cope with a more complicated combination of constraining forces including the courts, the media, provincial governments and special interest groups. The adequacy of these forces to hold the public service accountable has been profoundly affected by the growth in size and complexity of government, the increased technical content and nature of political decisions and the need for increased co-ordination and bargaining with provincial governments. These and other pressures have combined with the result that today, policy formulation is being left increasingly to the skills of the professional public servants rather than to our elected representatives. This development has contributed to unprecedented levels of criticism of the federal public service and of government bureaucracy. "Bureaucracy bashing" is strictures against the right of public service unions to bargain have of government bureaucracy in general and the public service in particular.

THE PERCEPTION OF THE PUBLIC SERVICE BY THE PUBLIC

A recent study of the image of the public service in Canada concluded that during the 1970s the government was perceived to have improved steadily, at least in terms of its fairness and promptness. But, despite this, the perception of most Canadians is that the public service still lags far behind the public sector in terms of efficiency and ability.[24] The study also concluded that direct contact with individual public servants, even when such contact is favourable, does not spill over and contribute to a favourable view of the public service.

The hostility Canadians feel for their public service was pointed up in a public opinion poll conducted during the deep recession of 1982. At that time, a high percentage of those polled supported the notion of punishing the civil service and the public service unions because they were not providing Canadians with "value" for their money.[25] The June 28th budget, which imposed wage controls on federal public servants, was partly a response to the popularity of this perception.

Since 1960, the bureaucracy has itself increasingly become the *object* of Canadian public policy. In this connection, the federal public service has been subjected to wage controls (1975 and 1982), macro fiscal policy, collective bargaining (1965), language policy, human rights legislation, freedom of information laws, "value for money" auditing and decentralization and relocation of government agencies. Problems and controversies regarding these policies coupled with a growing economic malaise have helped to alter the once favourable perception of the public service.

The growth of militant public service unions in the last decade has also contributed to the poor image of the public service. Unions such as the Canadian Union of Postal Workers and the Canadian Union of Public Employees have attracted a great deal of public and media attention and comprise a large part of the total membership of the Canadian Labour Congress. In Quebec, the public service unions have also become very powerful and have aligned themselves almost naturally with the fate of certain public policy matters—especially social programs in education, pensions and health, and transportation services. Thus, despite the theoretical a striking indicator of the unfavourable perceptions Canadians about matters of public policy, collective bargaining inevitably embraces considerations that relate closely to public policy.

Criticism of the bureaucracy must be carefully examined in the light of these considerations. It must also be linked to a realistic understanding of the role of the senior public service in the field of policy formulation.

CONTROL OF THE PUBLIC SERVICE: THE ELUSIVE GOAL

Governments have long struggled with the perplexing issue of how to use and yet maintain effective control over a burgeoning professional public service. Several attempts at reform have been made. For example, efforts to strengthen the Prime Minister's Office and the cabinet committee system made during the late 1960s were in part directed toward this end. During the 1970s, the criticisms made by the Auditor General with respect to financial practices in the public service resulted in several initiatives, including the appointment of the Comptroller General and the establishment of the Lambert Commission. Subsequent royal commissions, advisory committees, task forces, green papers, white papers, and appointments of ministers of state have all, in part, been intended to broaden the base upon which policy decisions are made and so reduce bureaucratic influence.

Despite such periodic responses to the general problem of public service accountability, an overwhelming majority of parliamentarians agree that the senior public service has too much influence over public policy. Evidence of this growing influence, however, is not easy to identify. Nonetheless, there is a genuine need to examine the extent to which the public service generates major policy initiatives as opposed to merely implementing the policy decisions of the government.

The real concern over senior public servants' influence on policy formulation stems not only from their ability to *initiate* policies but also from their ability to *frustrate* "official" policy (of elected ministers and political parties) by raising administrative hurdles or instituting tardy implementation schedules.

It is evident that senior officials are given considerable leeway with respect to initiating policy. To some extent, at least, Parliament expects and encourages them to do so by giving them wide discretionary powers to enforce and interpret statutes and to promulgate regulations that often embody and flesh out the pith and substance of legislation.

As to having the power to block policy, virtually every minister has a story to tell about a great idea that was somehow sabotaged by the senior bureaucracy. In most cases it is difficult, if not impossible, to determine why a pet ministerial project or initiative is changed or stalemated. In some cases there may be a difference in values and priorities; a deputy is sometimes able, by a simple wearing-down process, to impose his views upon his minister. In other cases, the deputy may merely be playing his proper constitutional role in warning the minister of the pitfalls of a proposal and the possible contradictions between it and the law. Occasionally, too, it is not the minister's department at all that stops a proposal going forward but rather other ministers whose concerns and priorities are at variance with the plan at issue.

Flora MacDonald's brief account of her nine-month ministerial experience as Secretary of State for External Affairs in the Clark government points up the wooliness of the question of bureaucratic influence.[26] She describes several ways in which officials employ "entrapment devices" for ministers (e.g. delayed recommendations, multiple deputy ministerial committees and bogus "options"). Miss MacDonald also describes the difficulties she experienced in establishing alternative advisory networks of academics in relation to her personal political staff. She is careful to say that her problems did not arise from the overt partisanship of senior public servants; public servants consider themselves to be above the partisan battle and she quotes approvingly, other experienced politicians on this point, from Tony Benn to Henry Kissinger. But nowhere in her account is there a specific example of a policy blocked or an initiative frustrated. The impression is simply that a problem exists—which should surprise no one.

Despite this, parliamentarians are genuinely complimentary about the way in which the public service handles day-to-day grievances and the problems of their constituents. The main concern of parliamentarians is focussed on senior public servants' influence on policy and their related responsibility for financial management.

SPECIFIC DETERMINANTS OF MINISTERIAL/DEPUTY MINISTERIAL RELATIONS

Relations between members of the public service and their political superiors ultimately crystallize in the day-to-day relations between cabinet ministers and deputy ministers. It is here that accountability is most crucial.

The policy-administration principle is a good starting point for considering relations between cabinet ministers and deputy ministers. In simple terms, the policy-administration principle is that *elected ministers should make policy and public servants should implement it* loyally, efficiently and effectively. The policy-administration principle draws a line (sometimes a blurred line) between: *policy enunciation and decision-making* and *policy implementation and administration.* The former is the preserve of ministers who are elected; the latter is the role of officials. This principle is an article of faith as well as an essential operating rule. As an article of faith, it is a constitutional principle and it makes a sharp distinction between ends and means. But there is much evidence to suggest that senior public servants do more than just implement policy. Nonetheless, there is little doubt that the belief in the policy-administration principle is an essential and powerful standard against which we judge the democratic policy process in Canada.

Federal and provincial governments alike have been concerned that the policy-administration principle is not only preached but is also practised. The Progressive Conservative governments under both Diefenbaker and Clark wrestled with this question when they assumed power after many years of Liberal dominance. They did not, however, act as forthrightly with respect to their concerns as might have been expected; instead they relied on the entrenched officials. The early Trudeau governments were also concerned, but took no significant action. At the provincial level, the election of NDP governments in Saskatchewan, Manitoba and British Columbia led to these governments questioning the loyalty of the civil services they inherited.

In practical terms, these problems centre on the day-to-day relations between a minister and his deputy minister. A minister must allocate his time, energy, and preferences to the many aspects of his portfolio, including:

- general policy development
- defending his department and the Government in the House of Commons, especially during question period
- cultivating media relations
- acting as a special regional minister

- developing relations with the caucus and the party
- acting as M.P. for his or her own constituency
- participating in cabinet meetings and on cabinet committees
- serving as the titular head of his department[27]

Specific allocations of time and energy vary according to the personality and abilities of each minister, his policy interests, electoral status (safe or unsafe seat) and the type and size of the department involved. Each minister is also assisted by a personal staff, technically known as exempt staff, who are concerned about his image and future political prospects as well as his present situation. Some ministers are more interested in their next cabinet portfolio than in their current one.

The deputy minister (and to a significant extent, other senior public service and political advisors, especially in the central agencies) is indirectly a part of the world of ministerial politics. Rarely is a minister allowed to choose his deputy. Nonetheless that deputy is expected to become an alter-ego to the minister. The deputy is responsible for the general management of the department and must also serve as one of the minister's main policy advisers, being fully cognizant of and sensitive to the political constraints and concerns of the minister. The deputy has a constitutional duty to warn and to advise the minister and an obligation to serve the rest of the government in a collective sense, just as the minister must. The envelope system introduced in 1979 now requires that deputies serve on "mirror" committees. Such developments bring additional burdens to most deputies (as well as ministers) in terms of meetings, and other responsibilities for briefing their ministers on wide-ranging decisions being considered by cabinet or its committees.

Within the framework of modern ministerial/deputy ministerial relations, it is becoming increasingly difficult to achieve an integrated cabinet with full government responsibility. Although most departments, agencies and crown corporations nominally report to or through ministers, there are different sorts of reporting relationships and hence different degrees to which ministers feel themselves responsible and deputies consider themselves accountable.

The evolving relationship between ministers and their deputies is often less of a superior/subordinate nature and more a matter of role differentiation. For example, some ministers have little taste for administrative and managerial matters; they prefer to allocate their time to their policy and political party duties. As a result, administrative matters are increasingly relegated to deputy ministers.

Many parliamentarians believe there is now a need to enunciate a formal doctrine of deputy ministerial responsibility to Parliament for the good conduct of administration. Even if such a doctrine were only informally acknowledged, it would result in more direct contact between the public service and Parliament.

The House of Commons Special Committee on Standing Orders and Procedure is currently studying what type of formal reporting relationship might be established between senior civil servants and parliamentary committees. Representations have been received from the secretary of the treasury board, the Comptroller General, the Auditor General and other interested parties. The issues involved have been dealt with recently by Senator P.M. Pitfield, who was Clerk of the Privy Council and Secretary to Cabinet— and as such, was Canada's most senior public service official. Senator Pitfield recognizes the need for reform and has called for "the public accounting by officials for acts within their competence." As a possible mechanism, he supports the adoption of "accounting officers"—senior officials at the deputy minister level who would account to Parliament for acts of administration attributable to their respective departmental officials.[28]

Former Prime Minister Joe Clark has examined what he refers to as the abuse of power by the senior public service.[29] He has spoken of "the arrogant abuse of power by zealots who use sympathetic or pliable ministers to impose their personal ideology on the Canadian Parliament and public." He cites the tax reform package in the November, 1981 budget—proposals that had been "languishing in the department of finance for years, waiting for a minister gullible enough to embrace them." He also refers to the introduction of the National Energy Program (NEP) as having been "concocted by a small group of theorists." Alleging that these were flagrant abuses of power by the appointed government, Mr. Clark discusses a more subtle and widespread problem—"Conscientious and able public servants regularly use their expertise to have busy ministers adopt policy positions without adequate study." Significantly, the former prime minister points out:

"Without anyone willing it to happen, our system has changed to the point where most policy decisions are taken by the public service, even if they are approved by the politicians. The appointed government decides more than the elected government does. That runs exactly contrary to the theory on which our system is based."

These views, sincerely held and strongly put, illustrate the emotion that surrounds the issue and may be tinged, perhaps, with a measure of political rhetoric. And yet, there is a growing consensus that if Parliament is to regain control of its decision-making processes, mechanisms must be established to ensure that senior civil servants are to some extent accountable to Parliament.

Another problem relating to the role division between ministers and their officials turns on the increasing specialization of the senior public service and the degree to which many public servants now tend to possess scarce expert knowledge. Given this scarcity, could not their background reports and evaluations of administrative matters and policy options be more widely circulated without unduly threatening the position of cabinet and the minister responsible for a decision? The rapid growth of policy and planning units in federal departments during the 1970s generated a large volume of analyses which is generally unavailable to Parliament or the public. The *Access to Information Act* may provide a legal mechanism that will be used to bring about wider circulation of these policy analyses.

Another source of strain in the relations between ministers and deputies stems from the frequent shuffling of ministers and deputy ministers. The argument put forward in the late 1960s was that a high turnover rate and a shuffling of deputy ministers would increase cabinet control of the senior public service because deputies would be less entrenched. However, the anticipated benefits proved to be negligible because the prime minister simultaneously decided to shuffle cabinets more often. Senior public servants argue that the game of "musical chairs" has had a negative impact on management and moreover, that it has caused both ministers and deputy ministers to adopt a "low profile-low risk" approach to their responsibilities to ensure their own survival. These patterns have been aggravated by numerous reorganizations of existing portfolios and the creation of new ones, each making it more difficult to pinpoint accountability and easier to evade responsibility.

Finally, Canadian authorities in public adminstration agree that a deputy minister must cater to several masters: his minister, the prime minister (by whom he is appointed on the advice of the

Secretary to the cabinet), and the treasury board and policy envelope committees (which exercise authority with respect to the general management and financing of his department). He must also respect the activities of the Federal Human Rights Commission, the Official Languages Commissioner, the Comptroller-General and the Auditor General. He is also subject to the multiple pressures and obligations that are part of the more embracing concept of collective ministerial responsibility.

Deputy ministers thus must cope with extraordinary and sometimes conflicting pressures. Over the past decade, as well as being general managers and policy advisers, they have been deluged with a seemingly endless stream of directives and reforms each of which may have been desirable separately, but which, cumulatively, have tended to distract them from their primary departmental responsibilities. Although the public service continues to perform its many functions well, and among knowledgeable people in Canada and abroad it enjoys a good reputation, there is little doubt that confidence in its effectiveness should be bolstered.

Deputy ministers quite rightly argue that as long as they are subject to conflicting and/or vague instructions from ministers, the cabinet, central agencies, special agencies of Parliament, and the many statutes they must administer, there can be no simple concept of accountability. Most agree that every deputy head must have a profound sense of personal integrity, a moral sensibility, and the self-assurance to be responsible and accountable to himself and others. At all times he must be prepared to render a public account for what has been done. He should be prepared to state that within the resources provided, the complexity of constraints applied, the vagaries, contradictions and absence of direction received, he has done his best to manage his department or agency and to carry out or do what he believes has been legitimately expected of him by government, his minister, and his peers. It is this ethic which is the foundation of a responsible public service.

Given the complicated network of forces that impinge on them and that must be reconciled, deputy ministers are correct to argue that they should be held accountable only for their general conduct or, if for a specific matter, only after all the factors influencing their decisions are taken into account. More stringent standards of accountability are appropriate only if deputy ministers are given correspondingly greater powers to perform their various functions.

It has been suggested that ministers should be permitted to appoint their own deputy ministers (subject perhaps to a veto by the prime minister). This would serve to constrain prime ministerial power as well as tighten each minister's control over his deputy. While this may seem a sensible suggestion, it would be achieved at the cost of badly needed interdepartmental co-ordination, since deputies might be more inclined to look "up" to their ministerial obligations rather than "across" to their obligations to other departments and to the government as a whole. A more practical suggestion that deserves consideration is that deputy ministers should be appointed by the prime minister in full consultation with the cabinet and each minister concerned. Where a new minister "inherits" a deputy through a cabinet change, the minister's preference with respect to the deputy should be given careful consideration by the prime minister.

A DOCTRINE OF DEPUTY MINISTERIAL RESPONSIBILITY FOR ADMINISTRATION*
It is difficult to devise new mechanisms for executive and public service accountability to Parliament. Nonetheless, the time is ripe for some experimentation. Even though policy enunciation and administration are closely intertwined, it is essential to find new ways to ensure greater accountability of the public service directly to Parliament. We sense a desire on the part of parliamentarians and a willingness among civil servants to reduce the anonymity pertaining to many of the activities of the public service. This can be achieved by making public more departmental documentation and by formally assigning responsibility for administration (especially financial management) to deputy ministers. Accordingly, we recommend that:

4. **A new doctrine of deputy ministerial responsibility to Parliament be established relating exclusively to matters of administration. The doctrine would set out the obligations of senior public servants and would include the obligation to testify before parliamentary committees on matters of administration.**

In addition to their continuing overall responsibility to their respective ministers, deputies should be required to answer regularly to Parliament through its committees. Critics of such an arrangement will argue that deputy ministers might become competitors

*We reiterate that the term "administration" in this context means policy implementation.

45

of their ministers, especially in the public eye. They will also argue that the loyalty of the deputy to the minister may be compromised and that direct accountability to Parliament for administration will remove the deputy from the minister's direct control. We contend that the benefits to be derived under such a system far outweigh the risks involved. It is our view that the impracticality of ministerial responsibility for the day-to-day operations of government departments must be faced.

It is generally agreed that ministers are heavily overburdened by their many responsibilities and that taking a lead on policy matters alone is a full-time job. According to one senior deputy minister, "Ministers must remain responsible to the House for policy decisions—we (deputy ministers) must accept responsibility for executing those decisions and we should be ready to account for their effective execution before parliamentary committees if necessary. This is the only way to make ministerial accountability meaningful."

Under the system being proposed, the testimony of deputy ministers before committees would be an everyday occurrence. Furthermore, regular, open contact between the senior public service and members of Parliament should lead to a more realistic understanding of the dilemmas of modern public service management, closer scrutiny of administrative practices and more precise pinpointing of accountability. This is not to suggest that under such a system ministers will not be involved in administrative issues or individual cases. Obviously they will be and should be. Where ministers do involve themselves directly in administration, it follows that they will be accountable for their specific decisions. Moreover, they will continue to be held accountable in Parliament by traditional means. Deputy ministers will also continue to offer policy advice as they do now.

A system that calls for deputy ministerial responsibility for administration represents only a slight modification of traditional parliamentary government. Nonetheless, it is an important and realistic reflection of the complex nature of modern government and public administration.

INCREASING POLITICAL CONTROL: POLITICAL APPOINTMENTS
AND A NEW MINISTRY SYSTEM

In addition to a new doctrine of deputy ministerial accountability for administration, three further complementary reforms are also suggested. The first is to increase the number and raise the level of senior public servants who are subject to order-in-council appointment by the prime minister. The second is to increase the number and raise the level of non-permanent advisers who are responsible to the prime minister and individual cabinet ministers. The third is to involve more elected representatives in the executive policy process by establishing a system of junior and senior ministers.

In each case the rationale for the reform is that it will encourage tighter political control of the senior public service, especially with respect to the development of policy.

Journalist Douglas Fisher accurately expressed the view of many parliamentarians in an article in which he reviewed speeches by Alvin Hamilton, a former Progressive Conservative cabinet minister and Senator Jacob Austin, a former deputy minister and now a cabinet member in the Trudeau government. "It has been unfair, almost crippling, that in-coming governments must accept without demur and not be able to make immediate, major changes of the highest-level officials who served the outgoing government and that these same officials should be anonymous, should not be criticized publicly, and should have assured tenure and rank."[30]

Fisher also supported Austin's rejection of the notion that deputy heads are "non-political" and "capable of serving political masters of different parties with the same intelligence, honesty and competence", and he agreed that the new prime minister should be able to recruit and appoint new deputies of his own choice.

Deputy ministers (and others of equal rank) are now appointed by order-in-council at the pleasure of the prime minister, but these positions are still occupied overwhelmingly by career public servants. Some parliamentarians recommend that these positions should become more partisan in nature and that such appointments should be extended to include assistant deputy ministers as well as deputy ministers. They suggest this could invigorate the public service and overcome the problems cited by Fisher.

There is consensus, however, opposing any broader use of partisan order-in-council appointments. Most object on the grounds that it would damage the merit system and the career concept in the public service without adequate offsetting benefits. We agree with this point of view. Our goal must be to strengthen rather than weaken the principle of public service neutrality. Accordingly, we recommend that:

5. The principle of public service neutrality be re-affirmed as the guiding factor in all senior appointments whether filled from within or from outside the public service.

There is support for the idea that the prime minister should appoint more "outsiders" from business, labour, and other sectors to public service positions. The present conflict of interest guidelines make this difficult, but some such step has to be taken to obtain an infusion of new ideas and to ensure that the senior officers of the public service are drawn from the best and widest pools of skill and experience. Experience with the Executive Interchange Program has, so far, not been entirely satisfactory. Business, labour, or other private sector organizations have been reluctant to make their best people available, especially when the problems to be dealt with are difficult ones. Their best people fear the risks involved in interrupting their service and the possibility of being overtaken by rivals. Too often, the unfortunate consequence has been that interchanges have been used as a convenient way to move unwanted people out of the organization. Clearly, the idea of interchanges is a good one and we believe it should be vigorously pursued. In order for it to work, however, private sector organizations will have to pay more than lip service to the idea and recognize that government experience can be a valuable part of an executive's career development.

The appointment of non-permanent senior policy advisers to ministers is an alternative to the politicization on a partisan basis of the senior levels of the public service by means of order-in-council appointments. These senior advisers should be chosen by the minister for their experience and strong generalist capabilities. They would provide the minister with the additional "eyes and ears" he requires to execute his ministerial responsibilities more effectively.[31] In most cases, these individuals would have, or be expected to have, a partisan commitment.

Ministerial budgets have recently been increased and authorization has been given to exceed the usual salary maximums for ministers' staff members in order to attract high calibre people. Support for this idea is based on the clear understanding that the responsibilities of policy advisers are *strictly advisory*. The fundamental premise is that advisers must not interpose themselves between a minister and his deputy minister. It is noteworthy that some ministers themselves do not support this notion arguing that they are already overwhelmed by advisers and would find it difficult to cope with and reconcile two conflicting sources of policy advice.

Commenting on this, an observer has noted:

"There is a good deal of potential value in ministerial assistants who are competent, independent, innovative and who share a sense of mission with their bosses. Ministers have failed to benefit from that potential for two apparent reasons: (1) they themselves have not attached importance to the recruitment of competent independent advisers who have a clear and important role, and (2) the prime minister and his advisers have been less impressed with the value of strengthening the position of individual cabinet ministers than they have with certain other central institutions of government.[32]

The appointment of non-permanent senior policy advisers deserves special attention because it provides the political arm of government with the additional resources so necessary to balance a strong and effective public service. A senior public servant in the central machinery of government put it this way:

"The problem with the perception that the public service is overpowering and unaccountable is due to the general weakness of the ministry and its political support systems. What we need are stronger and better-advised ministers bolstered by a more professional party apparatus."

There is also support for the idea of improving political control over the public service by involving more elected ministers in departmental policy-making processes. A system of junior and senior ministers could accomplish this. Junior ministers would be responsible for specific programs within a department and would be answerable and responsible to a senior minister and Parliament. Advocates in support of this arrangement argue that the current use of parliamentary secretaries and ministers of state could be adapted easily to this end.

None of the proposed reforms is entirely satisfactory. The addition of more junior ministers is not a new suggestion. Senior officials claim it would confuse customary reporting relationships between deputies and yield only more "jobs" for politicians. Ministers themselves tend not to favour the idea of adding more junior ministers to the present cabinet roster.

Much depends upon personal relations. Senior ministers want a say in who is assigned to them. Moreover, senior ministers do not want to be threatened by junior ministers. For their part, junior ministers find it very difficult to function in an atmosphere of continual uncertainty relating to their roles. Many parliamentarians object to the appointment of additional junior ministers simply because they are afraid it will increase the size of an already unwieldy cabinet and might contribute to a still higher turnover among ministers.

Although there has been much useful experimentation with ministry systems and cabinet organization in the past decade, it is our conclusion that the mere addition of more junior ministers is no longer likely to produce satisfactory results. In our opinion, there is more promise of significant improvement in accountability in adopting a ministry system in which a number of senior ministers have primary responsibility for policy development and co-ordination and junior ministers have a specific line or departmental responsibility. (Some parliamentarians claim that such a system already exists in a modified form in the cabinet committee on priorities and planning, and in the framework established by the board of economic development ministers.) We urge that a formal reconstruction of the ministry system, incorporating the senior-junior ministry concept, be given consideration and that special care be exercised to ensure that the composition of the senior ministry reflects the various regions and sectors of Canada.

The Clark government's brief experiment in 1979 with a formal "inner" and "outer" cabinet did not conform to this concept. First, the inner cabinet was a very small group and did not provide for full regional representation. Second, and equally important, the full cabinet met infrequently. There must be adequate opportunity for the full cabinet to meet if the system is to work properly and retain its legitimacy in the minds of other ministers, the party caucus and the country as a whole. In this respect, the Trudeau government, since 1980, has improved upon the Clark government's cabinet structure and envelope system.

To increase political control and to enhance public service and executive accountability we recommend that:

6. **Appointments at the deputy and assistant-deputy minister level be made with a view towards increasing the number of qualified non-career public servants in such positions.**

7. Ministers be encouraged to appoint personal policy advisers who will hold their appointments at the pleasure of the minister.
8. A full senior-junior ministry system be adopted that maintains a satisfactory regional representation in the senior ministry.

The trade-offs involved in securing any improvement in executive and public service accountability to Parliament become even more difficult to assess when they are related to the issue of prime ministerial power. Indeed, many parliamentarians consider the growth of prime ministerial power to be at the centre of the problem of accountability. Despite this, many of these same people are willing to accept the appointment of junior ministers and more appointments by order-in-council—both of which are the prerogative of the prime minister—even though they know this arrangement is likely to strengthen the prime minister's power even further.

There are no easy answers to these questions of accountability. Certainly, the views of prime ministers and their attitudes as to how and towards what ends accountability will be exercised, inevitabily influence what actually happens. Accountability is almost always a compromise between the main centres of formal and informal power. Leaders of opposition parties as well as prime ministers have been known to change their minds about accountability as soon as they came to power.

There is no one solution to satisfy all conditions for all time; preferences for strengthening various elements will shift as the complex and delicate balances in power are upset by the changing dynamics of governments and personalities. It is essential, however, that the *implications* of strengthening one or another of the elements in the system of public service accountability be clearly understood by everyone. There is a delicate interplay between the various components: the public service, deputy ministers, ministers, ministerial staff, the prime minister, the cabinet and Parliament.

The Accountability of the Executive and the Public Service to Parliament for Public Finance

ACCOUNTABILITY AND MODERN ECONOMIC MANAGEMENT
The power of the purse is considered by most authorities to be the

central mechanism by which Parliament holds the executive to account. The government alone is responsible for initiating a spending and taxation program. Parliament must accept, modify or reject it. It has therefore been established through convention that if a government spending proposal is rejected in the House of Commons, this shall be taken as an indication of non-confidence and the government must resign. Convention has also established that supply,—"the authority to raise and spend money"—is granted by the House of Commons and must receive legislative approval each year.

THE INADEQUACY OF TRADITIONAL CONCEPTS
The traditional concepts of public finance were developed at a time when the aims of public finance were relatively simple—to balance revenue and expenditure and to ensure honesty and probity in both the collection and expenditure of public monies. In addition, the management of public finance was consolidated in a central agency—the Department of Finance (and the Treasury Board). These ideas and arrangements were based on the expectation that, except in time of war, revenues and expenditures would balance. It was also presumed that the full financial process should operate on the basis of a one-year parliamentary timetable. To what extent are these concepts appropriate today? If the principles are still valid, should changes be made in their application?

In the years following World War II, significant new demands were made on government, the most important of which had to do with its economic responsibilities and the way in which it manages the economy. During the immediate post-war period, Keynes' theory of demand management was widely accepted. It suggested that *total* government taxation and spending could be used in a substantive way to stimulate or retard overall economic performance. In particular, it alleged that "stabilization policy measures" could be applied to "fine tune" the economy on a short-term basis (i.e. 12 to 18 months).

In the 1950s and early 1960s only one economic budget was presented to the House of Commons each year. By the late 1960s and early 1970s, however, Keynesian concepts were being challenged by the reality of simultaneous high inflation rates and unemployment. The combined pressure of these economic forces was eventually brought directly to bear on the government. Fiscal authorities felt it necessary, as a result, to present more than one economic budget per year, claiming that the economy required even more careful balancing and management. The government had to appear to be doing "something" about these problems.

Controversy still exists concerning the continued viability and usefulness of these post-war fiscal and monetary policy tools. What must be clearly recognized, however, is that post-war concepts of economic management have had an important influence on the government and how it approaches many of its other responsibilities. For example, many of the techniques associated with Keynesian economic management were believed to be equally relevant to the pursuit of social goals—particularly those in which the public expected government involvement. Keynesian theories were also considered by many to offer at least a partial alternative to more fundamental changes in social policy. And so, as major expenditure programs were developed in connection with unemployment insurance, manpower, education, welfare, and health care, the rules of economic management were inexoribly extended to embrace social and "supply management" issues. Many of these programs thus acquired twin objectives: to effect change in the social structure and to achieve long-term economic stabilization.

In the late 1970s, as the level of socio-economic expenditures was rising markedly, serious questions were raised concerning the extent to which programs can be controlled by such techniques. At the same time, the effectiveness of many individual programs was also challenged. Today concerns over effectiveness and control are substantially increased because so many programs involve so much federal-provincial co-operation and interdependence. More recently, the application of supply management principles has required governments to ensure that adequate supplies of essential commodities and services are available for distribution. Thus, energy, resource and food policies have increasingly become part of the economic management process.

There is also growing concern with respect to decisions made by government through its regulatory agencies (the CRTC, for example) since these agencies make significant "non-expenditure" decisions which profoundly affect budgets and decisions in the private sector.

THE NEED FOR A LONGER TIME-BASE
Clearly, more realistic concepts of economic management must be

integrated successfully into the Canadian system of parliamentary government. Events are forcing society in general, and governments in particular, to revise their planning bases. Expenditure and budgetary processes covering only one year are no longer adequate. A longer time-base for programs along with a broader range of objectives must be accommodated to achieve better control over public finance. The requisites of Keynesian economics and a contemporary concern for individual program evaluation have been added to the traditional concerns over fiscal integrity, honesty, and probity. It is also important to know more about the cumulative effects of such expenditure and regulatory activity on particular sectors of the economy. In this connection, choices must be made between capital investment and consumption expenditures that vitally concern business, labour, consumer, agricultural, and other economic groups.

Although the process has been very slow, many of these requirements have been accommodated, in part, through structural and departmental changes within the executive branch of the Canadian government. Little recognition of the fact has been evidenced by Parliament, however, in terms of parliamentary practice or machinery. The result is a serious loss by Parliament of any meaningful scrutiny of public finance.

Parliament is presented with a five-year fiscal plan but it only approves the estimates for the coming year and thus it continues to operate within a one-year time frame. It examines revenues and expenditures through entirely separate processes. It lacks an adequate base of information. Parliament, in short, has virtually lost its capacity to scrutinize the country's financial affairs and has abrogated its duty to hold the executive effectively accountable.

The inadequacies of the present Parliamentary system can be seen in sharp relief in the context of the two main components of a modern budget process—the expenditure budget and the economic budget. These are described separately but the need for the two to be considered together in any reform of parliamentary procedure is readily apparent.

THE EXPENDITURE/ECONOMIC BUDGET PROCESS

An individual minister with the help of his departmental staff, generally identifies, develops, and proposes alternative spending programs for his department. It is the responsibility of the cabinet as a whole to evaluate and select the programs to be acted upon and to assign priorities to them. Although this may appear to be a straightforward and simple process, it is on the determination of priorities and the evaluation of various programs' effectiveness that much of everyday politics is centered. Each year the government must decide how it will allocate available funds to existing programs as well as to new ones. Increasingly, such choices involve significant cut-backs or the complete elimination of existing programs in order to divert funds for other purposes.

The objectives of a government expenditure process are:
- to provide cabinet with the means of directing the total pattern of government expenditures towards the overall goals and priorities of ministers;
- to ensure that the allocation of resources to specific programs reflects these priorities;
- to permit a review of the performance and future prospects of the economy to ascertain whether emerging expenditure policies are consistent with the economic aims of the government;
- to ensure that specific expenditure proposals satisfy the government's objectives of priorities in the most efficient and effective manner and;
- to provide for the evaluation of existing policies and programs to determine which are ineffective or of low priority and which should therefore be deleted.[33]

This list of objectives contains provisions which experience has shown are in conflict with one another. This is largely the result of changing political priorities which reflect strong short-term pressures exerted by major economic interests and governments. A recent analysis of public expenditure evaluation confirms the conclusion drawn from earlier analyses that there are few real incentives to evaluate programs in accordance with the foregoing list.[34]

Important changes have been made recently to rationalize the priority-setting and expenditure process. The new process, which leads directly to the tabling of the annual estimates before Parliament and indirectly to the budget speech and taxation proposals, is referred to as the policy and expenditure management system (PEMS) or, more generally, as the envelope system.

The principles underlying the envelope system are:
- **Integration of policy and expenditure decision-making.** This ensures that policy decisions are taken in the context of knowing

what a program costs and how much is available to spend on it. Decisions so taken should also reflect an understanding of and responsibility for ministers' policies and priorities.

- **Decentralization of authority for decision-making to policy committees of cabinet.** This recognizes the increasing range and complexity of government responsibilities, the interrelationships of policies and programs and the primary responsibility of the cabinet committee on priorities and planning (to focus on the central strategic issues and overall priorities of the government).

- **Publication of a long-term fiscal plan.** This projects government revenues and expenditures over a five-year period and thereby identifies the overall resource constraints within which policy and program choices can be made.

- **Establishment of expenditure limits for policy sectors.** These "resource envelopes" set limits consistent with the long-term fiscal plan and government priorities. Appropriate policy committees of cabinet are responsible for the management of these envelopes.

- **Development of policy sector strategies by policy committees.** These provide an overview of a sector which should enable a government to adopt a particular approach for that sector and thereby integrate individual actions.

- **Regular reviews of existing policies and programs and their resource levels.** These are conducted within an adequate planning time-frame so that policy committees can re-direct resources to reflect the government's changing priorities.

- **Responsibility of policy committees for the management of envelopes.** This role (delegated by the cabinet committee on priorities and planning) ensures that proposals having policy implications are referred to the relevant policy committees for decision.

- **Responsibility of the Treasury Board for the integrity of the financial and other resource systems.** This includes accurate costings of present and proposed programs put before ministers as well as timely advice to ministers on the efficient management of public resources generally.

- **Integration of policy and expenditure advice within the locus of the policy committees.** This brings about collation of advice from the ministries of state, the treasury board secretariat, the department of finance, the privy council office, and other departments.

- **Timely sharing of appropriate information between all central agencies.** This ensures the effective functioning of the system.[35]

Implementation of these principles will require that:
- the role of cabinet committee chairmen be enhanced,
- direct expenditures and tax expenditures be included in the expenditure envelopes,
- support staff of cabinet committees (particularly the economic and regional development and social development committees) be strenghthened and expanded,
- parallel envelope committees of deputy ministers (which support cabinet committees) be further developed to bring about increased agreement between departments, ministers, and other officials.[36]

The main differences in this system, in contrast to the one embraced in pre-envelope days, are its longer time-frame and the onus it places on ministers to say "no" to each other more often than previously. Under earlier systems ministers could much more easily leave the problem of saying "no" to the president of the treasury board or the minister of finance. Under the envelope system, however, the cabinet committees must now function somewhat like "mini-treasury boards", at least in the sense of having to come to grips with the competing financial demands between departments contained in a single expenditure envelope.

It is important to note that the system ultimately depends on whether the priorities and planning committee (which is a cabinet committee and chaired by the prime minister) holds a disciplined line on the fixed amounts allocated to each envelope committee, and whether appeals are allowed. If the line is held, the system has a chance to succeed. If not, the system will be little different in practice than the one that preceded it.[37] Indications so far are that the new system is a significant improvement over previous ones. We support its introduction and continued development.

STAGES IN THE EXPENDITURE AND ESTIMATES PROCESS
The envelope expenditure system is, at present, the main mechanism for integrating the collective direction of cabinet with the individual spending proposals of ministers and departments. The workings of this system are summarized as follows:

- Expenditure blocks (envelopes) are assigned to cabinet commit-tees as shown in Figure 1. Each envelope allows varying degrees of discretion according to whether programs involve fixed trans-fer payments or other statutory commitments as noted in Figure 2. Figure 3 illustrates the main stages of the cycle.
- The minister of finance and his senior advisers prepare an economic outlook and fiscal framework review each fall, ap-proximately 18 months before the beginning of the target fiscal year (beginning April 1st).
- The priorities and planning committee, each autumn, sets the government's overall priorities, sets and reviews the 5 year fiscal plan and assigns policy reserves for each committee's envel-ope(s). A policy reserve can be positive (new funds available) or negative (new initiatives only if other programs are reduced or eliminated).
- Each policy committee prepares an overall sector outlook for its policy sphere. Planning guidelines are then supplemented and resources are allocated within the limits of the envelope and the reserve.
- Finally, the treasury board prepares an overall expenditure out-look, reviews department operational plans and manages the detailed preparation of the annual estimates to be sent to Parliament.
- In the early autumn, departments submit their detailed estimates to the treasury board. There, they are combined with other further resource allocation information based on decisions that have been approved by cabinet since July. By the end of Nov-ember, a draft of the main estimates is prepared. This is virtually the last point at which cabinet can substantially affect the level of expenditure for the target fiscal year.
- The document sumarizing the main estimates is printed during December and, by law, is tabled in the House of Commons not later than the end of February. The estimates are then sent for review to the relevant parliamentary committees. The new fiscal year to which main estimates apply always begins on April 1. Interim supply (approximately one-quarter of the estimates) must be approved by the end of March; the balance of the review lasts until late May when the estimates are approved. During the fiscal year, the government may approve further expenditures from the budgetary reserves. It may also alter spending in response to short-term economic considerations, cover "over-

runs" in statutory commitments, or accommodate crown corporation activities. These additional expenditures are submitted for parliamentary approval in the form of supplementary estimates.[38]

- Figure 4 provides an illustrative example of the cycle in practice from April 1980 to September 1981 for the target fiscal year beginning April 1st, 1982. Needless to say, every year is somewhat different depending upon specific circumstances and events.

STAGES IN THE PROCESS OF ECONOMIC BUDGETING AND TAX LEGISLATION

The expenditure process is tied indirectly to the budget speech and the tax legislation process that develops from the budget speech. This process normally begins with the preparation of an economic outlook paper by the department of finance and the development of the "Fiscal Framework" for the months ahead. The latter exerts a particular influence on how much "new money" for policy reserves the government will have to spend. Bearing in mind that there are often two budget speeches per year, the budget preparation and tax legislation process normally consists of three phases:

Submissions for tax changes.   The minister of finance and his officials receive submissions for tax changes from interested individuals and groups before work on the detailed budget begins. Submissions are made on a private basis without any prior indication given by the minister as to what alternatives he may be considering.[39]

Budget gestation.   The minister of finance, assisted by a select group of officials over approximately a six-month period, adopts specific budget proposals, which are reviewed by the full cabinet just prior to budget night. Budget secrecy is maintained during this period.

Parliamentary Phase.   This phase begins with the presentation of the budget in the House of Commons and the tabling of one or more notices of ways and means motions in which the proposed tax changes are summarized. The budget speech is delivered and the budget debate, lasting up to six days, ensues. The minister of finance then moves acceptance of his ways and means motion(s) and the bill(s) to amend the appropriate statutes is introduced and given first reading. Following second reading, the bill goes to a

FIGURE 1.

PRIORITIES AND PLANNING	ECONOMIC AND REGIONAL DEVELOPMENT	SOCIAL DEVELOPMENT	FOREIGN AND DEFENCE	GOVERNMENT OPERATIONS

Cabinet Committees and their Resource Envelopes

PRIORITIES AND PLANNING	ECONOMIC AND REGIONAL DEVELOPMENT	SOCIAL DEVELOPMENT	FOREIGN AND DEFENCE	GOVERNMENT OPERATIONS
FISCAL TRANSFERS	**ECONOMIC AND REGIONAL DEVELOPMENT** – Industry and Technology – Agriculture, Fisheries & Forestry – Regional Economic Expansion – Transportation – Communications – Labour, and Consumer and Corporate Affairs	**SOCIAL AFFAIRS** – Employment & Immigration – National Health and Welfare – Indian Affairs and Northern Development – Canada Mortgage and Housing – Veterans Affairs – Secretary of State – Environment	**EXTERNAL AFFAIRS AND AID** – External Affairs – Foreign Aid	**PARLIAMENT** – Senate – House of Commons – Parlimentary Library
	ENERGY – Energy, Mines and Resources – Oil Import Compensation Program – Home Insulation Program			**SERVICES TO GOVERNMENT** – Executive – National Revenue – Post Office – Public Works – Supply & Services – Statistics Canada
PUBLIC DEBT		**JUSTICE & LEGAL** – Justice – Solicitor General	**DEFENCE** – National Defence	

FIGURE 2.

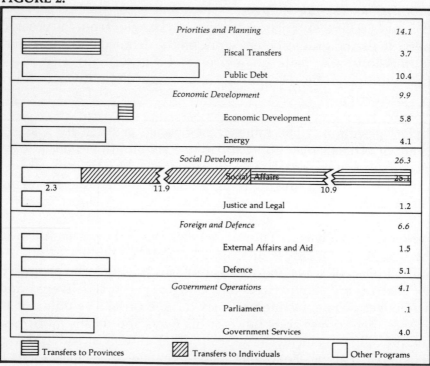

Priorities and Planning	14.1
Fiscal Transfers	3.7
Public Debt	10.4
Economic Development	9.9
Economic Development	5.8
Energy	4.1
Social Development	26.3
Social Affairs	25.1
Justice and Legal	1.2
Foreign and Defence	6.6
External Affairs and Aid	1.5
Defence	5.1
Government Operations	4.1
Parliament	.1
Government Services	4.0

2.3   11.9   10.9

Transfers to Provinces   Transfers to Individuals   Other Programs

FIGURE 3.

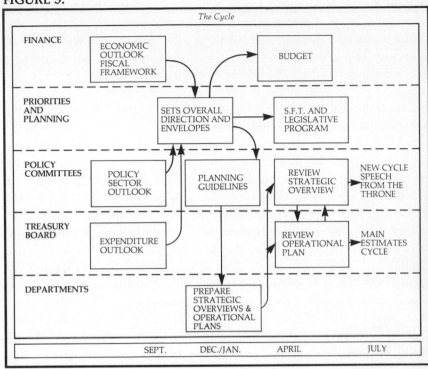

The Cycle

FIGURE 4.

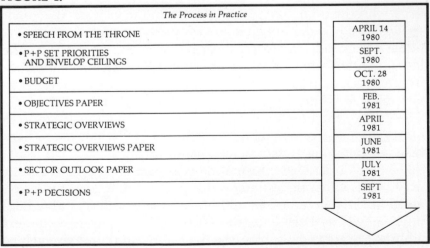

The Process in Practice

• SPEECH FROM THE THRONE	APRIL 14 1980
• P+P SET PRIORITIES AND ENVELOP CEILINGS	SEPT. 1980
• BUDGET	OCT. 28 1980
• OBJECTIVES PAPER	FEB. 1981
• STRATEGIC OVERVIEWS	APRIL 1981
• STRATEGIC OVERVIEWS PAPER	JUNE 1981
• SECTOR OUTLOOK PAPER	JULY 1981
• P+P DECISIONS	SEPT 1981

committee of the whole for a clause-by-clause analysis. At this committee stage no amendments inconsistent with the substance of the ways and means motion(s) may be moved. No witnesses are heard on the bill. Following the committee report to the House, third reading is given; Senate scrutiny then follows.[40]

THE INADEQUACY OF PARLIAMENT'S BUDGETARY/ECONOMIC MANAGEMENT INFORMATION AND SCRUTINY MECHANISMS

Until 1972 there were only two kinds of formal budgetary/ economic management information supplied to Parliament: the estimates "blue book", and the papers that accompany the budget speech. Of course, Parliament can also utilize information published by Statistics Canada and other government agencies and policy advisory bodies. Nonetheless, and despite several recent improvements, there is a consensus that the kind of information Parliament receives to assist it to scrutinize public finance is inadequate. In some instances, there is not enough information; in others, information is plentiful but not meaningful. It is also agreed that there is insufficient staff support to help digest information and to advise on what facts are not known or what information is being withheld. A brief look at the blue book and the budget papers illustrates the problems.

THE ESTIMATES BLUE BOOK AND THE ROLE OF PARLIAMENTARY COMMITTEES

The estimates blue book contains the government's annual main estimates. It is essentially a catalogue, by department, which sets out a general statement of the objectives of each program along with the total numbers of dollars and man-years (personnel resources) required. Though it lists the previous year's expenditure, it does not include any forecasts or retrospective analysis. Neither does it contain any evaluation of programs or assessment of how programs relate to each other or to the policies of the government. Nor does it comment as to trends in program expenditures. Nonetheless, the blue book represents the single most important information source available to members of Parliament to assist them in examining government expenditures.

The lack of detailed information was partially corrected in the early 1980s when the estimates documentation began to be contained in *three* volumes. In addition to the traditional blue book (now known as Part II of the estimates) a separate volume is published (Part I) describing the overall fiscal plan by envelope.

The five-year fiscal plan itself is set out in the budget speech and the new estimates blue book (Part II) relates the annual envelope expenditures to this plan. In 1982 Part III of the estimates was added. This new section, entitled Program Expenditure Plans, provides historical data and relates departmental programs to the overall objectives of government. Resources are justified and goals are set. As one might expect, there is little critical analysis of the data provided.* Despite these improved sources of data and analysis, the heart of the problem of scrutiny still rests with Parliament.

The procedures and structure of parliamentary committees were designed to allow for effective scrutiny of the estimates, but they have not been successful. The committees do not examine government policies and programs in any integrated fashion and they often ignore policy changes implicit in the annual estimates. Moreover, the success of departments in achieving their policy objectives or in executing their operations efficiently is not scrutinized at all carefully. The problem is aggravated by the attitudes of members towards their task.

As has been noted:

"This lack of enthusiasm for the scrutiny function is partly caused by the handicaps under which the committees work. All the estimates are tabled at the same time. The rush to study them and report before the deadline dates means that many committees are meeting simultaneously. Members find it impossible to attend all the hearings on the estimates that interest them or affect their constituency. Ministerial attendance is usually limited to several hours so that the time available for policy discussions is limited. Members do not have the spending decisions . . . Frequent turnover in the membership of committees means that many members lack the information to question officials effectively . . . The sporadic, uncoordinated and haphazard approach of the standing committees towards the study of administrative efficiency means that the managerial aspects of control are left largely to the Treasury Board, the Auditor General and the Public Accounts Committee.[41]

It is worth noting that there are several major inadequacies in, and disincentives to, the effective use of the information in committees

---

*Some independent critical assessment of federal expenditures is being supplied by the School of Administration at Carleton University, however. The School's annual publication *How Ottawa Spends Your Tax Dollar* contains an assessment of the fiscal plan and analysis of the expenditure of several federal departments and agencies.

and elsewhere. This persists despite the fact that significant improvements have occurred with respect to providing staff support to individual members of Parliament and the political parties.[42]

The Budget Papers.   The budget papers are those which accompany the finance minister's budget speech. They are a good example of "information overload". They represent another important area of financial activity about which Parliament is ill-informed. The budget papers have become increasingly complex and cumbersome documents. They reflect the complexity of the economy and are accompanied by virtually no summary materials that might shed light on short- or medium-term fiscal assumptions and the framework of the government's fiscal and monetary policy. The deficiency has been identified and the government now prepares for its own internal use a "medium-term track paper" on the state of the economy. Each year, policy sector outlook papers which up-date five-year projections and reviews, are also prepared for each envelope. These documents should be in the public domain. Accordingly, we recommend as a general reform that:

> 9. **More explanatory materials accompany the budget papers submitted to Parliament by the minister of finance.**

Tax Expenditures.   Information overload constitutes the main problem with the general budget papers. But there is another area related to "tax expenditures" where, despite recent improvements, the problem is the lack of useful information. Tax expenditures, in general terms, are revenue "losses" resulting from special provisions in the tax laws providing for preferential treatment. These include such items as the child tax credit provisions of the autumn 1978 budget and corporate fast write-off provisions (accelerated depreciation) of earlier budgets. Such expenditures are designed to give relief to individuals and/or to generate special incentives for individuals and corporations to pursue certain courses of action. Such tax provisions are considered expenditures in that they are revenues the government chooses not to collect.

A study by professor Allan Maslove contends that in Canada tax expenditures have been growing relative to budgetary expenditures and revenues, while in the United States the rates have been relatively constant, and that such tax expenditures are distributed heavily in favour of higher income groups, thus decreasing the progressivity of the personal income tax system.[43] Maslove attributes the increasing use of these tax expenditures in part to the fact that they are hidden and are therefore not as openly displayed as are regular budgetary expenditures. While there may be problems in accurately identifying such expenditures, similar concerns in the United States to those identified by Maslove led to the passing of the 1974 United States Congressional Budget Act which requires that the President's budget include a listing of such tax expenditures.

In 1979 the Honourable John Crosbie tabled a Tax Expenditure Account with his December budget speech. The Honourable Allan MacEachen continued the practice in 1980 and again in 1981. We consider the Crosbie intitiative to be very valuable. However, since there is no legislative basis for it, we can only hope that the practice of tabling a Tax Expenditure Account with a budget speech will be continued.

Two features of the tax decision process require comment.

The first is that within the federal government, the tax expenditure decision route is much shorter and less visible than the regular expenditure decision route.[44] The latter involves many agencies and elements of the cabinet and public service; the former is much more exclusively confined to the department of finance. The serious consideration here is that at a time when criticism of regular public expenditures is increasing, some special interest groups have an incentive to seek benefits (and the government may also be inclined to confer these benefits) via the more hidden tax expenditure route.

The second feature emerged clearly in the controversy that followed the MacEachen budget of November 12, 1981. Although the budget led to debate about several issues, our concern here is how it pointed up problems relating to the content of information in a tax expenditure account. The budget in question closed or reduced several areas of tax expenditure as a general revenue raising measure. Coming at a time of severe economic recession, these changes aroused unprecedented criticisms, particularly from the business sectors most affected. The tax expenditure document as it is structured at present cannot possibly capture the policy importance of the tax measures proposed in relation to the particular policy fields and industries concerned (e.g. insurance, housing) because it does not effectively disaggregate them enough or relate them to parallel expenditure policies that show up only in the estimates blue book. Clearly, further changes in the Tax Expenditure Account are required and so we recommend that:

10. **The minister of finance be required to publish with the budget additional data on tax expenditures showing in detail the connection, by program, between the tax expenditures and major direct expenditures in each program area.**

NEW INFORMATION AND FORUMS FOR PARLIAMENTARY SCRUTINY

Everyone must be realistic about the capacity of Parliament to utilize more information. There is considerable room for improvement in the type and quality of information now being provided. However, change will occur only if the government is committed to the view that Parliament has a legitimate right to influence and to criticize economic management policies. At present there is no (committee) forum in which the total expenditure budget or medium-term expenditure plans and projections for the next three to five years can be evaluated. Nor is there a forum in which related revenue and taxation matters can be assessed. Similarly, there is no mechanism for judging programs or the relations between closely associated programs of more than one department. In terms of both the macro and micro aspects of public finance, the existing system is therefore deficient.

Parliament is in need of significant informational reform. Hal Kroeker, a former senior policy advisor in Ottawa, contends that Parliament needs all of the following kinds of information:

• a general assessment of past and future trends in government expenditures covering a span of ten years—five years into the past and five years into the future;
• a description of the economic basis upon which future projections have been made, e.g. expected rates of growth in GNP, rates of unemployment, inflation, increases in wage rates, etc.;
• comprehensive overviews of departmental programs along with an indication of how these relate to other programs and the government's policies.

Kroeker's view is that the assessment of past and future trends in federal finances will enable members of Parliament to discuss the broad implications of these trends and to understand better the underlying forces and policies that trigger changes in these patterns. Such aggregate trends are of interst to the general public and should ideally be broken down on a functional basis into such areas as regional development, energy and cultural expenditures. In some cases this would necessitate breaking out some components that are not now identified.

It has also been suggested that such information on trends include projections showing how various statutory and formula-based programs can be expected to affect expenditure levels and what factors can be expected, over time, to accelerate these expenditures. In addition, MPs and the public would have a better understanding of some of the broader assumptions concerning economic policy if the economic rationale upon which expenditures are projected were included. The blue book, therefore, would become a series of volumes containing analysis of past and future trends of government expenditures, the economic data upon which these trends are projected, and the traditional department-by-department listing of expenditures. As noted earlier, the changes made to the blue book since 1980 now provide some of the data advocated by Kroeker.

In addition, Kroeker recommended that new data be given to Parliament in the form of departmental five-year overviews. Such a departmental "green book" (or whatever other colour may be chosen) would complement the estimates blue book and would fulfil a number of requirements such as identification and explanation of the policies to which a department's programs relate; a statement of how each minister views the relationship of his programs to these policies and to other relevant government programs, and five-year expenditure and manpower projections, by program. Such a compilation would concentrate on the next year or two and would enable Parliament to see how ministers view their mandates and what they are trying to accomplish as a government. It could be prepared to coincide with the examination by Parliament of departmental estimates. Since Kroeker's recommendations were put forward, the government has instituted a system of Departmental Multi-year Operational Plans (MYOPs) which contain some of the information recommended. These documents are prepared by each department for submission to the treasury board at the end of March. An updated version accompanies the main estimates when they are presented in October. The information in these plans is available to members of committees but the question is whether or not members have the time, expertise or staff support that would enable effective use of the data.

Substantive reviews utilizing this detailed information would require much improved parliamentary committee work including adequate research support, greater stability in the membership of committees, and the calling of witnesses from both within and outside government to give testimony. (Public servants would provide technical information and information relating to the implementation and funding of programs but they would not be called upon to make judgments concerning policy.)

While we share the view that "green book" or MYOP information must be developed, we also believe it must be done on a selective basis. Experience with respect to program evaluation both inside and outside government is at best undeveloped. Program evaluation, moreover, must not be carried out on a narrow accounting basis. Evaluation must take into account the multiple and changing purposes of programs and the need to develop a proper time frame for such evaluation. Some public programs cannot and should not be evaluated on a short-term basis. Nonetheless, they should all be subject to the rough and ready test of electoral acceptability, even though it is recognized that most individual public programs are not the object of electoral scrutiny by the Canadian people in any single election.

With regard to aggregate expenditures, it has been suggested that Parliament should debate, and a new central expenditure committee of the House (or the Senate) should scrutinize, an annual white paper on public spending. This is the practice in the United Kingdom. Such a document would project expenditures for the next three to five year period. It would not be a "planning" document, but rather would make public some of the data and information already used by the government in its internal deliberations. The federal government's five year "fiscal plan", published annually since 1980, could easily serve as the basis of such a document. It is extremely doubtful that any fiscal plan as it is originally constituted would, in the face of uncertainties, turn out to be a plan *per se* but there is no doubt that it would bring about more focussed debate. For this to be achieved, a specific forum in Parliament would be required.

Not surprisingly, parliamentarians are not unanimous in their support of these recommendations for new kinds of information. Some officials stress the substantial costs and difficulties involved in their preparation and question whether they would ever be used. However, the 1978 throne speech committed the federal government in principle to making available to Parliament information on program evaluation. Some members of Parliament are suspicious of any officially produced information; they prefer to have their own staff prepare their own evaluations or have them provided by more independent outsiders.

The idea of a white paper on public expenditure is questioned by a few who are skeptical as to the reliability, and hence the value of projections over even three years. Still others question whether politics and the partisanship inherent in a Parliament dominated by party discipline will ever allow or induce Parliament to focus on the medium-term future as opposed to the here and now.

Another point of serious concern has to do with the inadequacy of the current estimates process in assessing the financial affairs of crown corporations.[45] The expenditures of crown corporations are only partly reflected in the blue book in the form of net capital requirements, and there is precious little information in their annual reports. In any case, there is no proper forum for their consideration and review.

The issue of parliamentary and executive control and scrutiny of crown corporations is both important and difficult to resolve satisfactorily. There are many types of crown corporations with widely varying mandates. They enjoy different degrees of independence from the cabinet in matters of personnel, capital, operating budgets and policy. Many operate as autonomous commercial entities, albeit with a sensitivity towards their public role and broad public policy objectives. Increasingly, however, concern is being expressed by cabinet ministers as to their accountability for the activities of crown corporations, especially when a ministerial portfolio includes several such corporations.

The lack of scrutiny by Parliament when new crown corporations are established is now the source of intense public concern. Such concern is legitimate. Many subsidiaries of existing crown companies have been created without formal approval by Parliament; Via Rail was brought into being through the slippery device of a "dollar vote" in the estimates. The Canada Development Investment Corporation (CDIC) was established in 1982 without Parliamentary approval. The omnibus energy policy legislation passed in 1982 contained carte blanche powers to establish crown corporations without further reference to Parliament. Collectively, crown corporations constitute an important segment of government activity and of the Canadian economy yet they are subject to only intermittent scrutiny by Parliament. Crown corporations are the object of special concerns arising from their independence and their diverse sources of revenue. They require a separate parliamentary forum for scrutiny. Accordingly, we recommend that:

11. A standing committee of the House of Commons be established to investigate and scrutinize the finances of selected crown corporations each year.

Parliamentarians agree that virtually the only area in which successful financial accountability is effectively pursued is in the public accounts committee assisted by the Auditor General's office. Although the size of the Auditor General's staff is subject to treasury board approval and has from time to time been cut back, it still affords the public accounts committee a greater degree of independence than any other committee. The committee is chaired by an opposition member and has developed many non-partisan traditions. It has not, however, achieved the degree of persistent non-partisan scrutiny that its British counterpart enjoys. The work of the public accounts committee in the United Kingdom is aided by the practice of designating deputy heads of departments as "accounting officers"* with legal obligations to defend their financial management practices before the public accounts committee. There is thus a more direct accountability link between the committee, the executive, and the senior public service in the United Kingdom than there is in Canada.

There is no doubt that the role of the Auditor General is central to the system of financial accountability to Parliament. However, as mentioned earlier, there is genuine disagreement over the proper limits of that role. The Auditor General argues persuasively that there is a need to achieve better "value for money" and that he should play a role in assessing whether the proper "systems" are in place. (He attempts to distinguish between systems and evaluation but, in fact, this may be a distinction without a difference.) Controversy has also arisen because in practice this tends to involve evaluation of government policy as well as administra-

---

*See earlier by Senator Pitfield, page 42.

tive efficiency. Douglas Hartle of the University of Toronto, has quite properly questioned the right and the capacity of the Auditor General's staff to evaluate issues that are basically of a policy and political nature. He argues that it is preferable to assign such responsibilities directly to Parliament and its elected members, assisted by staff with backgrounds broader than those of accountants and finance specialist.[46]

We contend that there is conclusive evidence to show that, on several points, Parliament lacks both information and proper forums in which to scrutinize public finance. We therefore recommend that:

12. **The minister of finance and the president of the treasury board be required jointly to publish an annual white paper on government expenditure. Such a document should contain information on expenditure plans and projections over a three- to five-year period, on a departmental and program basis as well as on the basis of economic category of expenditure. The document should also include a projection of revenues for the same time period and information on the government's medium-term economic forecast and the assumptions underlying it.**

13. **The white paper on government expenditure be presented to Parliament late in each calendar year (prior to the presentation of the blue book estimates) and that a one-day parliamentary debate follow that presentation.**

14. **A new standing committee on the expenditure budget be established to receive and scrutinize the white paper and to invite testimony on its contents.**

15. **Four departments and agencies—two selected by the opposition parties and two by the government—each year be required to submit to Parliament a departmental "green book" evaluation of its programs, such evaluations to be tabled at the same time as the estimates blue book.**

We consider these changes to be essential complements of a strengthened committee system and a reformed legislative process.

They would strengthen the information base upon which accountability for departmental programs, total government expenditure, and relations between expenditures and revenues must be founded. Along with our other proposals they would enhance the degree to which tax decisions and policies, and tax expenditures, are openly scrutinized and debated by members of Parliament and others. Above all, these new informational requirements would help to induce a greater concern for the medium and long-term consequences of current expenditure choices and policies. It is also important to stress that we view these changes as further means by which the executive and Parliament together, can become more effective in managing and scrutinizing the public service.

PRE-TAX BUDGET CONSULTATION AND TAX LEGISLATION

One of the most striking manifestations of the inadequacies of present parliamentary (and extra-parliamentary) practice exists in the tax policy-making and legislative enactment process.[47] Criticisms of this process can easily be traced back to the early 1960s and the Carter Commission. Criticism reached its peak, however, with the controversy in the wake of Finance Minister Allan MacEachen's budget in November 1981. Ministers of finance, businessmen, tax specialists, and interest groups all voiced objections concerning the inadequacy of pre-budget consultative opportunities and about the increasingly complex and numerous tax amendments that accompany budget speeches. For example, it has been estimated that tax reform legislation of 1971 required approximately 175 amendments by the time it passed the House of Commons and Senate. The budget of 1973 required 175 amendments. The 1974 budget required 146; the 1976 budget, 75; and the 1977 budget, 95.[48] In 1976, this concern led the minister of finance, Donald Macdonald, to commission a study of the legislative process as it applies to taxes. That study was carried out by the Canadian Tax Foundation and published in November 1977. It recommended a number of ways in which broader participation and consultation on tax and budget matters could be achieved.[49]

To date, no discernable action has been taken on this report nor has any substantive action followed the tabling of a green paper by Allan MacEachen following the debacle of the November 1981 budget. (The proposals contained in the MacEachen paper were much more limited than those advocated by the Canadian Tax Foundation.)

Current Dissatisfactions Dissatisfaction with the tax process today is literally nation-wide. Ordinary citizens and special groups can write or send submissions to the minister of finance, but there is no requirement that these be made public and there are few opportunities to discuss tax proposals with the minister. Even finance ministers complain about the severe constraints of budget secrecy; several of them have reported that in the six months preceding the budget speech, their own knowledge of the probable impact of alternative budget proposals could be enhanced by more consultation with affected groups and industries. Tax specialists complain that without pre- and post-budget consultations it is impossible to prevent the many technical difficulties that characterize recent tax legislation. There is also concern about the uncertainty of the meaning of tax provisions which must be implemented on short notice. Most members of Parliament feel frustrated because they have virtually no opportunity to influence a process that directly affects all Canadians. Finally, the excesses of budget secrecy inhibit federal/provincial tax co-ordination.

Similar concerns arise in relation to all tax processes, including those that follow from legislation and policies normally deemed to be non-economic. The Tax Foundation study attempted to distinguish between major tax policy changes (e.g., incentives for the mining and resources sector) and changes in the machinery or structure of the tax system (e.g. rules about corporate surpluses). Both types of change require lead time and the maintenance of secrecy (to eliminate any risk of private gain). Both suffer from inadequate consultation. The study stated that:

> "Throughout, the procedures respecting tax legislation . . . are conducted in a manner which limits effective input by persons other than the minister and his relatively small group of advisers. Prior to the budget speech, the notion of budget secrecy operates to limit the opportunity for public debate on alternative policy options; after budget night, the procedures in the House limit the extent to which defects in the proposed legislation can be identified and cured during the legislative process."[50]

Ideas for Reform The Tax Foundation study recommended reforms that take into account the legitimate need for budget secrecy. The recommended reforms also recognize that it is the minister who is ultimately responsible for the government's fiscal and tax policies, and that his mandate must be sufficiently flexible to permit him to handle and respond to complex interdependent economic management problems. The proposed reforms are:

- That a subcommittee on taxation of the Standing Committee on Finance, Trade and Economic Affairs be created (supported by expert staff and resources) to which major proposed changes in tax policy should be referred for study through the aegis of a green or white paper.
- That general ideas for fiscal policy should be referred to the subcommittee in order to invite public and parliamentary input, unless advance knowledge of such proposals would provide those apprised of them with an opportunity for private gain.
- That, where time or other circumstances make the foregoing suggestion impractical, the Minister of Finance should announce that he or she has certain policy options under consideration and invite comment from interested parties, subject to the more constrained concept of budget secrecy. Such intentions should be announced in the House of Commons. Where possible, the reference to the subcommittee or the solicitation of outside comment should include the terms of any legislation required to implement the proposed change.
- That, on a trial basis, the tax bill enactment process should be changed so that complicated structural provisions (e.g. corporate surpluses) can be considered in a standing committee following second reading, either by dividing proposed legislation into two bills or by adopting rules that will permit a single bill to be split so as to allow structural clauses to be considered in a standing committee.
- That, on a trial basis, the convention that most tax changes become effective as of the date of a budget speech be reconsidered. Structural tax changes would then come into effect only when a bill passes. This should be the case except where fiscal policy or equity considerations require that the changes be effective as of budget night.[51]
- The Tax Foundation study group also recommends that the minister of finance provide more explanatory information on first reading of the bills—a point noted in our earlier discussion of the inadequacy of Parliament's information.*

*See earlier section re Budget Papers, page 64.

Most parliamentarians support in principle the idea of more extensive and more open pre-budget consultation, but some have reservations about more open consultation in practice. The concern expressed most often is that consultation is likely to be dominated by groups with the time and money to participate. A few cited their experience with the white paper on taxation in the early 1970s. At that time it was felt that the consultation process favoured those who were against the more egalitarian provisions of the white paper. A study by Audrey Doerr of Simon Fraser University tends to confirm this view.[52] Others doubt that the minister of finance would, in practice, be inclined to heed such consultations.

The proposals contained in the autumn 1978 budget to reduce abuses in the use of personal incorporation is an example that elicits contradictory reactions; some opposed pre-budget consultation in this instance because they felt it would water down a desirable tax change; others argue the benefits of consultation in applying pressure against a bill which, in their view, contained many unfair provisions.

The events following the controversial MacEachen budget of November 1981 point up the dilemma of consultation. The government "acted" first and "talked" later. Their move to reduce several tax expenditures (variously called loopholes, incentives, and tax breaks) was justified in part as a social policy tax reform measure to create greater equity in the tax system. Had they consulted first, it is likely that the special interst groups would have prevailed at the outset. Instead, the government acted first and was then forced to back-track on its position as the affected groups mounted lobbying efforts that were without precedent in their vigour. Which approach yields better results—"consult first—act later" or "act first—adjust later"? There is no easy answer. Both approaches pose problems for the government and for the interests affected—those who can afford to participate and those who cannot.

Unquestionably, additional opportunities for consultation on tax matters would be seized enthusiastically by many special interest groups. But that is part of the objective. The decision-making process is now very closely—too closely—confined. Major reforms are needed to allow for consultation and scrutiny by a wider range of experts and interested parties. It is a difficult but essential part of every politician's and government's function to weigh the sources of their advice as well as the substance of the advice they receive.

Opening the budgetary and economic management process to broader parliamentary scrutiny will not be achieved easily. Members of Parliament are generally ambivalent about the balance between openness and secrecy. The 1963 Gordon budget was criticized in part because the then minister of finance used outside advisors. Finance Minister Chretien's 1978 sales tax budget aroused controversy because it involved pre-budget consultation with the provinces. Ambivalence aside, however, we believe that more open consultation is needed, both prior to a tax budget and during the ensuing legislative process and that Parliament should play a prominent role in the consultation process. Accordingly, we support the main suggestions made by the Tax Foundation study. In particular, we recommend that:

16. **A joint House of Commons-Senate committee on economic policy be created and that it be co-chaired by a government member and an opposition member. The committee's task should be: to hold pre-budget hearings; to receive testimony from the minister of finance, the president of the treasury board, and the governor of the Bank of Canada; to receive and scrutinize the annual reviews of the Economic Council of Canada; and to hear testimony from such non-governmental experts and organizations as required.**

17. **A subcommittee of the House of Commons standing committee on finance, trade and economic affairs be established to conduct an ongoing review of major changes in tax policy.**

18. **Members allow the structural and technical provisions in a tax bill to be separated from the bill during the legislative process and scrutinized by an appropriate parliamentary committee.**

By way of elaboration on the first recommendation, it is clear that while the budget debate is undoubtedly an occasion of great importance, Parliament as a whole lacks an adequate forum for discussion of budget, tax, and economic policy issues. The late Dr. John Deutsch of Queen's University was among those who urged Parliament to establish a central committee on economic matters to deal with the budget and to receive and scrutinize the reports of the Economic Council of Canada. (The latter body has no formal relationship with Parliament at present.)

The model of the Joint Committee on Regulations and Other Statutory Instruments (which is co-chaired by representatives from the House of Commons and the Senate) seems to be a good one in that it encourages a balance between partisanship and detached objectivity. We envisage the committee holding brief televised pre-budget hearings in which key economic ministers and officials and outside experts would be called to testify. The committee can also serve as a forum for public scrutiny of the annual reviews prepared by the Economic Council of Canada.

We do not believe that this sensitive and important task can be handled effectively by existing or other proposed committees. The present House Committee on Finance, Trade and Economic Affairs has a heavy agenda and would have an even heavier one if our proposal (that it have a subcommittee to review ongoing major changes in tax policy) is accepted. Similarly, our proposed committee on the expenditure budget would have its time fully occupied. The Senate Committee on National Finance might appear to be an appropriate forum since it is largely detached from partisan politics, but we are reluctant to recommend only a Senate forum; we belive the House of Commons must be involved in this central task.

The recommendations that we have put forward for improving both the scrutiny of the expenditure process and the participation of Parliament in the budget process have been examined by the House of Commons Special Committee on Standing Orders and Procedure. Two members of the committee, the Honourable Ronald Huntington and Claude-André Lachance have adopted many of the suggestions in their submission to the committee, *Accountability: Closing the Loop*. The Special Committee is expected to make recommendations in the near future that will (if implemented) . . . "dramatically change the financial, administrative, and ministerial accountability of the government and senior public servants to Parliament".[53]

In conclusion, if the scrutiny of public finance is at the heart of the notion of accountability in parliamentary systems of government, then it also strikes at the heart of Parliament's current weakness in holding the executive and the public service accountable. Whether viewed from the expenditure or revenue side, or in relation to the modern demands of Canadian economic management, the parliamentary role in the accountability process needs strengthening.

The Legislative Function of Parliament

THE ROLE OF PARLIAMENT IN LAW-MAKING

A significant part of Parliament's time is devoted to examining and judging how, and how well, the cabinet and the public service administer the affairs of the nation (the accountability function). But it is Parliament's role as a law-maker that is paramount in the minds of most citizens. Yet the legislative function of Parliament is often misunderstood. Within the areas of federal jurisdiction, it is true that a statute of Parliament is supreme in that it takes precedence over all other law. However, Parliament is not the only law-making body in the federal context. Statutory law is augmented by the cumulative decisions of the courts; by orders made by the Governor-in-Council (the cabinet); and by rules, regulations and decisions made by ministers and a variety of other regulatory bodies under authority delegated by statute. Theoretically, all law originating from sources other than statute law passed by Parliament expresses the will of Parliament. If this were not so, Parliament would take appropriate action to resolve perceived conflicts.

Members of Parliament, as members, do not have the *primary* responsibility for making law. The onus for the initiation and content of new legislation rests primarily with the executive. Each session of Parliament begins with a speech from the throne which, in effect, tells members why Parliament is being convened. The practice dates back to the first parliaments in the thirteenth and fourteenth centuries and demonstrates that members have been summoned primarily to consider the financial requests and legislative proposals of the Sovereign's ministers, rather than to introduce their own bills.[54] Also, today, it is upon political parties, leaders and party programs that the Canadian electorate bestowes a mandate; voting for an individual member is simply a means of accomplishing this end.

The dominance of the legislative process by the executive within the Canadian parliamentary system is to-day virtually complete because of the growth, relative to Parliament, of the power of the executive and the public service. Decisions as to what shall constitute a legislative program during any particular session are made outside Parliament—by the cabinet and its public service advisers. Almost all bills that become law are government bills (i.e., initiated by the executive) and tend to be altered very little in the House of Commons or the Senate. This has led to intense, ongoing debate as to whether and how some degree of balance should be restored to the legislative process that will allow members of both the House of Commons and the Senate to play more significant roles in the initiation and development of legislation.

THE ROLE OF THE INDIVIDUAL MEMBER

Individual members have a three-part role to play in the parliamentary process; to deal with the problems and grievances of their constituents, to participate in the development of legislation and, to exact accountability from the executive. The "ombudsman" role tends to occupy a large part of a member's time, often at the expense of his other functions. It is a critical part of a member's responsibility to represent those who elected him, not only by voicing his opinions on matters before the House, but also by attending to individual problems and complaints. With the establishment in 1974 of constituency offices at government expense and the hiring of constituency secretaries to aid members, the volume of constituency business has increased substantially. There are two reasons for this increase: constituents want to exert more influence on the formulation of policy; and the number of government services and programs has increased, so there is simply more opportunity for problems to develop. In any case, the very nature of politics demands that members keep in touch with their constituents and election workers in their home ridings if they hope to retain their seats.

To help members cope effectively with their constituency and parliamentary business, changes were implemented in the late 1970s to improve staff support. A new classification system for staff employed in members' offices allows members to hire up to three full-time staff for the Ottawa office and one full-time secretary for their constituency offices. Although this has indeed been a great help, most members still find it difficult to allocate their time satisfactorily. Many resolve the conflicting demands made on them by giving priority to their constituents. As one member points out "The constituent's problem is there in a very concrete sense . . . responsibility for answering the constituent and for trying to deal with the problem cannot be transferred beyond the MP's office."[55] It is generally agreed that if members are to contribute significantly to the legislative process, they need and should have additional staff support, particularly at the constituency level.

Some members complain that the mechanisms and procedures within Parliament used most often to present grievances on behalf of constituents (e.g., written questions to ministers, Question Period, the "late show", and motions previously put pursuant to Standing order 43—now "Members' Statements") are inadequate. Unquestionably, there are grounds for dissatifaction, but there is no consensus among parliamentarians as to how the situation might be improved.

LEGISLATIVE ACTIVITIES: PRIVATE MEMBERS' BUSINESS

Parliamentarians become involved in the legislative process in two ways. First, as members participating in the legislative program of the government of the day, they are involved in scrutinizing, proposing amendments, supporting and opposing government bills or helping to influence policy by receiving testimony and making recommendations on green papers, white papers and other matters referred to special committees by order of the House. Second, as private members, they are involved in initiating debate and introducing their own bills on chosen subjects during time set aside in the House for private members' business.

The importance of private members' business has declined steadily from the early days of parliamentary government when it occupied the majority of the House's time. Today, despite recent efforts to effect improvements, it has been characterized as "essentially a relic from bygone days at Westminster."[56] Bills sponsored by private members may deal with virtually any matter, but they must not require any expenditure of public money or reduction in revenues. Time is another major constraint that limits private members' initiatives. Under the previous House rules, only one hour per day, four days per week, was allotted to private members' business (subject to detailed restraint provisions). Under the new House rules (implemented for a one-year trial period commencing December 22, 1982) the time for private members' business is consolidated on one day per week (Wednesday) but is reduced from four hours to three (3:00 p.m. to 6:00 p.m.).

The time limits and rules governing the order and conduct of business during private members' hours determine that some bills and motions never come up for debate and most of those that do never come to a vote. The government can always control private members' time by having items "talked out" or defeated, illustrating again the extent to which it is the executive, not private members, that is responsible for governing the country. The value of private members' business is mainly that it provides members with an opportunity to speak in the House and thereby have their ideas and proposals appear on the record and before the public.

Many members, particularly newly-elected ones, tend to be unaware of the opportunities they now have to raise issues. They could make much better use of motions than they now do. To assist members, Beauchesne's *Rules of Procedure* has been simplified in the fifth edition. But this is not enough, and we concur with many parliamentarians who argue that the rules of the House should ensure that a certain number of private members' bills do come to a vote during each session.[57]

We recommend, therefore, in order to provide greater scope for individual members that:

19. Fifteen private members' public bills be allowed to come to a vote in the House in each session.

A feasible model upon which to base this recommendation is the Westminster private members' draw, which permits twenty members' names to be drawn from a hat for the opportunity to introduce bills. The model has been adopted in part by the Commons in that a draw is now used to assign precedence for public bills and notices of motion. Precedence is assigned but there is no guarantee that a vote will be taken.*

The recommendation that private members' bills be revived as a way of permitting individual members to play a more significant role in Parliament complements previous recommendations that serve the same end (that a group of 50 members of Parliament, ten drawn from each of the two political parties, be empowered to have a committee investigate any subject they agree warrants investigation; and that standing committees be empowered to investigate any subject within their jurisdiction).

Some members of Parliament contend that with enhanced legislative responsibilities they would require additional staff assis-

---

*Part of the House rule amendments effective December 22, 1982.

tance. Some suggest that in addition to their present staff complement of secretaries and one administrative assistant they should have specialized legislative assistance. Others argue against the provision of specialized legislative assistance on the grounds that the Library of Parliament now provides such services. At present, the research branch of the Library of Parliament, which has a professional staff of 53 researchers, represents the main source of legislative assistance available to the members and committees of both Houses. The Library, through the information and reference branch and the research branch, provides members, upon request, with substantial help in organizing, summarizing and analyzing information. Unquestionably, the Library of Parliament provides members with useful assistance. Nonetheless, some members would benefit significantly from having staff under their direct supervision. As one member pointed out, "I could use a bright legislative assistant who understands the legislative process inside-out, who feels a commitment to my views and needs, and who could provide me with first-class analysis in accordance with my direct instructions. The problem with the Library is that you often have to wait your turn and then the analysis is non-partisan."

A few members are satisfied that their respective party research facilities (caucus research bureaux) provide them with adequate partisan assistance. (The bureaux were created in 1968 at Prime Minister Trudeau's initiative and today each boasts a substantial budget: Liberals— $601,000; Progressive Conservatives— $541,000; and New Democratic Party— $285,000. Figures are for 1982-83.) Most members, however, disagree with this view, arguing that, while party research is generally useful, the assistance is not sufficiently specialized for legislative purposes and "often suffers in quality and speed of execution because it is being shared among so many".

The issue of what constitutes adequate staff assistance is not easy to resolve mainly because members' needs vary so much. The Clerk of the House of Commons described the situation accurately:

"Central to a determination as to the adequacy of staff in Ottawa is an understanding that different members have different priorities. Nearly all members combine to one degree or another their roles as legislators, committee participants, ombudsmen, and other work in various functions in their constituencies. Evidently, the emphasis differs from person

82

to person and, consequently, the needs in terms of staff must be adjusted, not only on the basis of constituencies previously outlined, but on the interests of the individuals concerned and of their constituents. As well, habits of work and personal industry, or the lack of it, are part of the equation."[58]

We are of the view that individual members of parliament would benefit from additional legislative assistance and that this assistance should be made available to members at their discretion. Accordingly, we recommend that:

20. **The staff budget for a member's Ottawa office be increased to allow a member, at his discretion, to hire one additional assistant to aid him in carrying out his legislative responsibilities.**

LEGISLATIVE ACTIVITIES: GOVERNMENT BUSINESS
The voting behaviour of the members in the House of Commons will, of necessity, always be responsive to the need to support or oppose items on the basis of party affiliation. It is only in caucus and in committee that members have an opportunity to influence the government's legislative initiatives.

THE ROLE OF CAUCUS
In 1969, changes in the government caucus system provided members of the government party with an opportunity to discuss the principles of most government bills prior to their introduction in the House. Ministers must now indicate on documents going to cabinet whether or not they have consulted caucus about them. Government backbenchers speak enthusiastically about the effectiveness of this innovation. Opposition members similarly participate in the development of their parties' policies and positions during their caucus meetings.

THE ROLE OF COMMITTEES
It is in committees that investigative inquiries, studies of policy matters and detailed examinations of bills referred by the House are carried out. Most government bills (other than appropriation bills, bills to change tax laws, and very simple bills) are now routinely referred after second reading, to the appropriate standing committee for detailed clause-by-clause scrutiny. Ministers and public servants (with their Ministers' permission) can appear

before committees to explain and support legislation and, if a majority of the committee so wishes, outside witnesses can also be called to appear or submit written briefs. However, at this point in the legislative process, attention is supposed to be restricted to the text of a bill as distinct from its ends or purposes. Debate on the purpose of a bill usually takes place before committee study (i.e. on second reading or subsequently, on third reading).

The committee stage is the key phase of the legislative process but it is also the focus of a multitude of complaints. One observer remarked, "to attend a meeting of a parliamentary committee is to be depressed for days."[59] Criticism is rooted in the fact that committee activity is still very much influenced by party discipline. Most committees, as a result, are not what most members hope for—dispassionate forums where sound advice and thoughtful amendments (obtained from private members from all parties) can alter the shape of bills. The hard reality is that strong pressures are applied by ministers and whips to influence committees' decisions. If, despite these efforts, committees persist in effecting changes the government does not want, the government can simply reverse them later in the House. Because their labours seldom generate results, there is a sense of frustration and futility among both opposition and government party committee members and a consequent decline in the time and effort many are willing to devote to the examination of bills in committee. One veteran committee member summarized his frustration thus, "I get no credits for committee work either from my constituents or the public. I often spend many hours trying to come forward with some useful improvements but generally the government is not interested. The work is boring and largely meaningless."

REFERENCES TO COMMITTEE

Many parliamentarians support an innovative practice that would remedy these problems—the referral of bills to committees, without debate, immediately after first reading rather than after second reading. The objective is not clause-by-clause scrutiny of a bill (to which the government is committed in virtually every detail) but something more akin to the exploration and examination of a white paper—a practice in which some committees are already engaged. Ministers and their public service advisers could explain and be questioned on the purposes and main provisions of bills. Outside experts and concerned parties would have an opportunity to be heard on the subject matter of bills rather than just on specific clauses. The government could better guage the likely reaction of the public as well as Parliament to bills and make modifications and improvements to them before moving second reading. Under such an arrangement, Parliament would be familiar with bills before debate on second reading and debate before second reading could, therefore, be more focussed and less protracted. This would overcome the criticism, voiced by virtually all parliamentarians, that debate on second reading is indiscriminate and wasteful of Parliament's time. Referring bills to committees after first reading would have the added advantage that committees could begin work on the government's legislative program early in each session. This, of course, would require government to have a significant portion of its program ready at that time. If the government were prepared to experiment with this proposal it could gradually, rather than precipitously, work toward the goal of having a large part of its planned legislation prepared for the beginning of each session.

The government's past use of white and green papers (when it wanted to consult systematically and freely with the public and Parliament about major policy areas before drafting legislation) is praised by parliamentarians. When these have been referred to committees of the House of Commons, the Senate, or joint committees of both, members have usually risen to the occasion. They have put aside narrow partisanship, moderated the influence of party discipline, and taken the opportunity to contribute in a constructive and substantive way to policy formulation.

The differences between white papers, green papers, exploration of bills by committee after first reading, and the committee stage after second reading are merely differences of degree. The cabinet is less committed to or constrained by the contents of green papers than of white papers. It follows logically that the cabinet is also less committed to the provisions of white papers than those of bills after first reading, and by the clauses of bills after first reading than those of bills after second reading. There are corresponding differences in the ability of individual members to influence the form and content of government policy or legislation and consequent differences in the strength of party discipline appropriate to each sort of endeavour. It is these facts that underlie the recommendations contained herein that committees be used more regularly and imaginatively for both pre-legislative consultation and legislative scrutiny.

Some progress has been made since 1979 with respect to the use of special parliamentary task forces—now called special committees. Task forces have consisted of a small number of MPs who are able to travel, gather research, and consult with interested Canadians on a variety of subjects (including handicapped and disabled Canadians, a national trading corporation, alternative energy sources, regulatory reform, equalization and financing of established programs, and labour market policies). They have been an extremely useful experiment. It must be noted, however, that the Government is under no obligation whatever, to state its position or to respond to the recommendations of a task force. Clearly, the task force experiment should lead to the next logical step, namely a much strengthened committee system. We contend that committees should be strengthened to perform two basic roles more regularly and effectively; to advise the cabinet on public policy and the soundness of legislation, and to serve as watchdogs over the cabinet and the public service in their administration of statutes and programs and the expenditure of funds. We concur with the majority view among parliamentarians that stronger committees and more substantive roles for individual members do not constitute a dangerous move towards a congressional system or to a weakening of our parliamentary system whereby the executive bears responsibility for the way it governs. Committees, as we envisage them, are not decision-making bodies, but will permit elected representatives to exert more influence on the government of the day. The floor of the House will continue to be the proper place for debates (indeed better informed debate as a result of better committee work) and final votes.

Specifically, we recommend that:

21. **The government permit individual members to play a greater role in policy formulation by more frequently preparing and referring to committees white papers and green papers on major areas of public policy.**
22. **Parliament experiment actively with the referral of bills to committee without debate after first reading.**
23. **In order to facilitate recommendation 22, the government be required to produce a major portion of**

its legislative program, including draft bills, early in the debate on the Address in Reply to the speech from the throne.

24. The House leaders routinely attempt to reach agreement on distinguishing major bills from minor bills, and that major bills be sent to committee after first reading.

SIZE AND MEMBERSHIP OF COMMITTEES

During the course of this study we isolated two main impediments to the efficient operation of the committee system.

First, there were *scheduling problems*—too many committees meeting on the same day(s). This caused conflict for members who wished to serve faithfully on two or more committees. It also made it difficult to maintain a quorum and so proceed with the taking of votes in committees.

Second, there were *too frequent changes in committee membership*. In order to ensure that the government party is not out-voted in committee because some of its members were absent (because of a timetable conflict, for example) whips substituted other party members as they saw fit. This meant that people unfamiliar with particular committee work were in a position to influence its recommendations. It also meant that the cabinet (through the whip) could remove party members who were not behaving in what it considered to be a sufficiently loyal fashion. Frequent membership changes were also disruptive; they impeded a sense of common purpose as a committee attempted to understand a piece of legislation or work its way through a set of estimates.

If committees were more frequently involved in considering green and white papers and examining bills after first reading, their work would (as we have argued) be less constrained by party discipline and the government would not have to be so concerned about maintaining a majority at all costs. However, there are times—as when, for instance, the texts of bills are considered *after* second reading, when matters which are potentially embarrassing to the government are investigated, or when opinions divide along party lines because of strong philosophical reasons—when the government will want to ensure that the activities and reports of committees reflect the majority view.

A compromise was needed.

We note with some satisfaction and approval that the recent

provisional changes to the House rules sought to correct both of these problems. First, committee size has been reduced from the normal 20-30 to something in the range of 10-15. Secondly, a formal and more restrained mechanism for substitution of members has been introduced. A Striking Committee will now prepare a list of alternates (equal in number to the members on a committee, proportional to the parties represented). An alternate member can act only in the absence of one of the regular members from his own party and can only then be counted in the quorum. In the interests of all concerned, there should be a working understanding between all members of a committee that no members will press for unexpected votes. However, in a crisis, a committee's ability to proceed with a vote can still be undermined by members choosing to leave, thus destroying a quorum.

If committees are to become effective forums for serious, less partisan consideration of proposed legislation and public policy, the roles and attitudes appropriate to chairmen must be re-examined. Constructive work is far more likely to occur if a chairman gains and maintains the general respect and confidence of all committee members and there is a feeling of mutual trust among members as work proceeds. At present, the view most generally held by committee members is that chairmen are the leaders of the government forces, ostensibly elected by a committee from among government members, but in reality chosen by the minister (or prime minister) to defend his interests or risk being removed. A certain impartiality is desired—one that permits a chairman to regulate debate between opposing factions and resolve procedural wrangles.

Peter Dobell, Director of the Parliamentary Centre of the Institute for Research on Public Policy contends that the government would pay much more attention to committee recommendations on policy if there was support across party lines for the position being promoted; therefore, if Parliament is ever going to be in the position to contribute to policy development, committees must strive to achieve a consensus that transcends party affiliation. He writes:

"... it is normally the chairman who builds a consensus ... to do this job effectively, chairmen need to feel that they (have) some independent standing ... Without the guidance of a sensitive chairman in every small decision relating to the work programme, mutual confidence and constructive activity will not develop . . . The trick is somehow to gain some independence of the government, while at the same time retaining the confidence of the ministers affected that their vital interests which the committee temporarily has in its hands will not be jeopardized . . . These are not common skills and even those with talent must learn from experience.[60]

To promote these ends we recommend that:

25. **Committee chairmen be elected on the basis of their leadership skills (not because of their loyalty to the government) by a simple majority vote of the committee members.**
26. **Chairmen be routinely re-elected as long as they continue to provide satisfactory leadership.**
27. **In order to make the position of committee chairman as attractive to a member of Parliament as the position of parliamentary secretary now is, similar remuneration should be attached to both positions.**

The last obstacle standing in the way of more effective committee work is the lack of adequate staff to help with the substantive work of committees—to help handle the planning of hearings, contacts with interest groups and experts as witnesses, analysis of important briefs, and preparation of reports and/or amendments. However, it is also recognized that the workload of many (not all) committees is sporadic and unpredictable so that having permanent staff attached to committees could be wasteful. Moreover, the amount and type of help required varies over time, depending on the particular tasks of committees. At present, committees can call on the research staff of the Library of Parliament for help. They also have the right to employ outside specialists, as needed, on a contract basis. If committee work is to become more important, as members bring their individual minds and talents to bear on policy formulation, scrutiny of bills, and efforts to hold the government to account for spending and administration, then an efficient way must be found to provide the staff support needed. Some committees could no doubt benefit from permanent staff immediately. Others will continue to require a flexible arrangement to suit their changing needs.

Accordingly we recommend that:

28. A study of the likely staff requirements of a strengthened committee system be undertaken as soon as possible.

The objectives of such a study would be to make competent staff available who are familiar with government and committee work when the need exists, to keep them usefully occupied at all times, and to meet non-recurring needs for specialist skills on a contract basis.

THE USE OF HOUSE TIME

The allocation and employment of House time is a critical issue in any discussion of parliamentary reform.

We note with approval the recent adoption by the House of Commons (for a trial period of one year) of a semester system whereby Fall, Winter and Spring sessions are defined with fixed dates. Under the new rules, the Speaker, after consultation with the government, retains the power to recall Parliament at any time if the public interest so requires and the royal prerogatives of prorogation and dissolution are preserved.

Also, reforms have been instituted in the daily parliamentary timetable to provide for more efficient use of members' time. We believe the changes are a positive step and in the main, we expect the trial period to prove the advantages gained. However, we question whether or not a fixed term for Parliament will prove manageable. Will the government be able to achieve its legislative goals when faced with an arbitrary summer adjournment date of June 30th? We hope that all party co-operation will permit the system to operate effectively.

Arguments favouring a fixed term are based on the expectation that parliamentary "management" will be vastly improved and that the government will be compelled to plan its legislative program more effectively and to use the time available to better advantage. We dispute this, however. Indeed, many parliamentarians feel that a fixed term unduly fetters the capacity of the government to govern, and moreover, comes far too close to creating a congressional form of government. An alternative approach that Parliament sit for *a fixed number of days* each year has much more merit in our opinion.

In 1968, the House Committee on Procedure and Organization recommended that parliamentary sessions should operate on the basis of five-week cycles: each five-week cycle to consist of three weeks of regular sittings followed by one week of committee hearings and one week of adjournment. This arrangement would allow members time to deal with constituency business, and cabinet ministers time to attend to ministerial business. The House Committee on Procedure and Organization reviewed the question of time again in 1976 and concluded that 150 sitting days a year, in addition to 15 days for committee work, was sufficient time for Parliament to be convened.

If the new reforms governing the use of House time do not prove to be acceptable or practical to implement in a "fractious House", we believe other alternatives should be tested to bring about greater order and stability to the business of Parliament. In our opinion, the Special Committee on Standing Orders and Procedure has an acceptable alternative. We recommend for consideration that:

29. **The House of Commons sit for a maximum of 150 days a year, plus the number of days needed for committee work.**

30. **Parliamentary sessions operate on the basis of five-week cycles, each cycle consisting of three weeks of regular sittings, followed by one week of committee hearings and one week of adjournment to permit members to carry out their constituency work.**

Many members of Parliament expressed deep concern about the length and effectiveness of debate in the House. One veteran member stated: "Debate has gotten out of hand . . . it is too long, it is too repetitive, it is too virulent, it does not do the job." There is, unquestionably, a willingness among members to curtail the length of debate and to accept stricter discipline from the Speaker on the issue of relevance. We therefore note with approval that the provisional House rules will now provide for a time limitation of 20 minutes on most speeches (down from 40 minutes) followed by a 10 minute question period designed "to promote a series of exchanges to enliven the debate and add a constructive element lacking in a debate simply consisting of a series of set speeches.[61] The Speaker is to have discretion in managing the 10 minute question and response session and with the co-operation of members, the quality of debate in the House will improve.

As a final word on reform of the Standing Orders (House rules) which govern the proceedings of the House of Commons, the work of the House of Commons Special Committee on Standing Orders and Procedures deserves a great deal of praise. The work of the special committee is little understood by the average Canadian and has little appeal as a means of garnering political recognition for a job well done. And yet perhaps no other committee will have as great an impact on the critical questions of governance that are now being faced in Canada by our primary democratic institution—Parliament. The fact that some of the committee's recommendations have been accepted by the government indicates a belief in a non-partisan approach to the problems and recognition of a sincere effort to introduce reforms that will balance the rights of government and opposition parties—a balance that will permit the government to govern and yet require it to account to the House for all its actions.

THE PROBLEM OF DELEGATED LEGISLATION

Our examination of the legislative function of Parliament has pointed up a concern on the part of many parliamentarians about delegated legislation—"one of the most complex problems of contemporary constitutional law".[62] As government has grown, so has the number of matters with which Parliament must concern itself. In order to deal with its legislative burden, Parliament has been forced to delegate much of its authority to the executive in the form of enabling legislation.* While this delegated authority remains within Parliament's legislative sphere, the extensive use of delegated legislation has substantially reduced Parliament's legislative role. Furthermore, because subordinate legislation often has policy implications, responsibility for the initiation, formulation and determination of policy has become even more the preserve of the cabinet and the executive.

Legislative power is normally delegated to the cabinet, a minister, an independent board or commission, or a combination thereof by way of enabling statute. This power is then executed in the form of various statutory instruments including rules, orders, regulations, ordinances, directives, forms, tariffs of costs or fees,

*Between January 1, 1969 and September 14, 1977, a total of 6,861 *Statutory Orders, Regulations and Other Instruments* were published.

letters patent, commissions, warrants, proclamations, by-laws and resolutions.[63] The important distinction between statute law and regulation is that Parliament has a hand in shaping the form and substance of laws before they are passed; regulations, which in essence provide the supplementary details of the parent statute, are normally drafted by officials of the department from which the legislation originates.

Delegated legislative authority and the regulations that result from it are sometimes a source of difficulty for both Parliament and the individuals or institutions to whom the rules apply. (The extensive review of facets of regulatory reform by the Economic Council of Canada has drawn attention to these problems.)[64] A major area of concern has to do with the degree to which the bureaucracy and federal boards and commissions are able to make decisions and take action free of political control or direction. Theoretically, every agency of government is responsible, financially and in terms of policy, to the cabinet or another appropriate legislative body. In practice, however, several federal boards and commissions wield substantial regulatory power with little or no cabinet or ministerial direction. Some MPs contend that the power to enact regulations is frequently abused. Some even suggest the wider use of "sunset clauses" as a way to limit the duration of enabling legislation and ensure the periodic review and re-evaluation of regulatory bodies.

Another major problem is the lack of a procedure for assessing the indirect costs and benefits of regulations on the economy. In April 1978, a private member's bill was introduced in the House, titled *An Act Respecting the Cost to the Public of Government Regulation.*[65] The purpose of this bill was to require that a document be tabled annually in the House that would cite the increased costs of products and services resulting from government regulation. Since then, the need for such an act has been raised again by several parliamentarians who feel that Parliament and the public have a right to judge whether or not the benefits of government regulations are worth the cost.

These problems have not been solved within the framework of the internal decision process of the government, either. A system of Socio-Economic Impact Analyses "the SEIA process" was started in 1978 but it applied only to regulation in the "health, safety and fairness" fields of social regulation under certain specified statutes. The envelope system, moreover, does not adequately come to grips with the assessment of regulatory decisions.[66]

Another problem arising from the delegation of legislative authority centres on federal regulatory agencies themselves. Individuals who are dissatisfied with an action taken by a federal regulatory agency have only two courses of review available to them: if the grievance has to do with the agency's interpretation of the law, they may seek a decision through the courts; if the complaint has to do with the substance of an agency decision, they can appeal to the cabinet. The difficulty is that the cabinet is being called upon increasingly to review decisions of regulatory bodies without being able to assure interested parties and the public that its rulings on appeals are fair and informed. Thus, the cabinet is free to consider all facts and arguments in an appeal—or none of them—which often causes even more problems for the parties affected. Some members suggest that, if the actions of the cabinet are truly an extension of the regulatory process, the clearly defined procedures applicable to regulatory agencies should also apply to the cabinet. Other members contend that the cabinet should not sit in appeal of regulatory decisions; but that if it must, then the cabinet's intervention should be public, debatable in the House of Commons, and subject to the approval of the House.

Ultimately, the most serious problem posed by regulations has to do with their ineffective scrutiny by public and parliamentary bodies.

PUBLIC AND PARLIAMENTARY SCRUTINY

The Standing Joint Committee on Regulations and Other Statutory Instruments, to which all statutory instruments stand permanently referred (as set out in Section 25 of the *Statutory Instruments Act*) has expressed the view that regulations should be subject to public scrutiny and debate. At present, members of the general public who are affected by regulations and other statutory intruments do not have formal access to those regulations until they are published in the *Canada Gazette.* This does not allow for adequate or sufficient scrutiny. Neither the *Canada Gazette* nor printed regulations are easily accessible to the average citizen. Furthermore, a large number of regulatory instruments do not have to be pubished in the *Canada Gazette* at all, either because they do not fall into the category of regulation as defined in the *Statutory*

Instruments Act, or because they are exempt from publication under one of the Act's exceptions. For this reason, it has been suggested that there should be a 60-day period between the time regulations are formulated and the time they go into effect. This would allow everyone who is affected by new regulations time to scrutinize them. Some parliamentarians argue that regulations should be prepared *before* the enabling legislation is tabled in the House, so that they can be considered simultaneously. Such a reform would not only save House time, it would also allow members to consider the full implications of the legislation. It is important to achieve a balance between the comprehensive knowledge of the person who has drafted regulations over a long period of time and the limited knowledge of an individual member who is expected to scrutinize regulations exhaustively within a short time frame. At the very least, members agree that where possible, departments should have all pertinent regulations drafted prior to the consideration of the parent bill in committee. As one parliamentarian has pointed out, ". . . regulations and the bill from which they originate go hand in hand and should be considered together in the same committee."

The sheer volume of delegated legislation makes it very difficult for Parliament to scrutinize effectively the exercise of regulation-making authority. Regulations are subject to a procedure prescribed by statute. They are reviewed in draft by the Crown's lawyers after formulation but before registration and publication; they are also scrutinized by the joint committee after promulgation. Other statutory instruments, however, may never be examined by anyone. Furthermore, the criteria by which the legal advisers to the Privy Council Office scrutinize draft regulations are less numerous and more restricted than those used by the joint committee in their scrutiny of the same regulations. With regard to this question, the joint committee stated in its second report that the distinction between "regulations" and "statutory instruments" should be removed. There would then be only one class of document defined under the *Statutory Instruments Act*. This would also mean that all law-making and rule-making carried out by the Crown and its agencies (or any other delegate of Parliament) would *in principle* be subject to parliamentary scrutiny.

Some parliamentarians are critical of the justice department's scrutiny of delegated legislation. They suggest that the standing committees should supplement the supervisory function of the department of justice by reviewing the delegation of authority—particularly regulatory powers—both before and after the fact. This suggestion derives, incidentally, from the fact that during its review of regulations, the department of justice is entitled to raise questions concerning both the form and the substance of a regulation. However, a shortage of legally trained legislative draftsmen tends to limit the department's review to matters of drafting form only.[67] Under the suggested arrangement, standing committees could specialize in their areas of concern and would be able to scrutinize the substance of the regulations alongside the parent statute.

There are signs that the open scrutiny of regulations in other standing committees (especially related to economic costs and benefits) may become more commonplace. For example, under the provisions of the federal Treasury Board's "Socio-Economic Impact Analysis Program" (SEIA) major new regulations in the fields of "health, safety and fairness" will be evaluated. Such evaluations are likely to be summarized and pre-published in Part I of the *Canada Gazette*, along with the proposed regulations. Eventually, each full evaluation will also be available and will be subject to scrutiny over a 60-day consultative period. This will allow sufficient time to meet with affected interests before regulations are promulgated.[68] This development is applauded, although there are several problems associated with the process. First, it is puzzling why it applies only to health, safety and fairness regulations and not to other areas. Second, it presupposes a capability in the committees which does not now exist—which merely reinforces the obvious need to strengthen committee staff support and the independence of the committee process.

Another positive development on the regulatory reform front is the recent establishment by the president of the treasury board, Honourable Herb Gray, of a system of regulatory agendas—documentation issued by the major regulating departments and the federal agencies that will give the private sector (and members) advance notice of regulatory initiatives being undertaken. The purpose is to provide "an early warning system" so that interested parties can make their views and critical comments available to the officials who are considering promulgating new regulatory measures. The commendable objective is a more open federal regulatory regime and higher standards of draftsmanship—simplicity, precision and practicality.

Although the subject of regulation is admittedly complex, we are strongly persuaded that two changes can and should be adopted immediately to achieve greater parliamentary scrutiny of delegated legislation. We recommend that:

31. **The draft regulations (delegated legislation) contemplated for a new bill accompany the new bill when it is presented to Parliament, thus permitting the joint committee on regulations and other statutory instruments to comment on the draft legislation.**

32. **The provisions of draft legislation granting regulation-making powers should automatically be referred upon second reading to the standing joint committee on regulations and other statutory instruments for study and comment.**

33. **The distinction between "regulations" and "statutory instruments" be removed from the _Statutory Instruments Act_ to enable a more complete scrutiny of all subordinate rule making by Parliament.**

THE ROLE OF THE SENATE IN THE LEGISLATIVE PROCESS

Although it is not much appreciated publicly, the legislative role of the Senate* is held in almost universal high regard by members of the House of Commons. One member of the cabinet recently stated, "we have the Senate to thank for refining legislation—we have some of the best minds in the country at work there and their record in improving bills is excellent."

It is also clear that the potential of the Senate to play an expanded legislative role remains unfulfilled. The reasons vary from simple benign neglect by the government and the House of Commons, to focused opposition by a few elected members to the idea that their non-elected colleagues should have any significant say in legislative matters.

In our opinion, the potential of the Senate in relation to the legislative process in Parliament should be developed by both the government and the House of Commons. The excellent record of the Senate in scrutinizing and improving government bills should encourage even more references to its standing committees. Its equally impressive record in developing useful recommendations concerning government proposals at the white paper stage also

---

*See also Section III, _Senate Reform and Regional Representation_, page 101.

suggests to us it should have a more significant role in the pre-legislative process.

There is an overriding need for everyone to recognize that a heavily burdened House can more effectively draw on the ample resources of the second chamber—particularly its experience and its time—and, in the case of its committees, the benefits of a largely non-partisan approach towards solving problems and resolving issues.

MEDIA COVERAGE OF THE LEGISLATIVE PROCESS

Media coverage of the legislative process today is of vital importance to parliamentarians and citizens alike. As one member points out, "the outside world . . . sees and understands Parliament through the efforts of journalists and broadcasters—they are largely responsible for the public's perception of what we do and how well we do it." Not surprisingly, therefore, many MPs express concern about the adequacy of media coverage of parliamentary activities. Their criticism tends to focus on the superficiality of the analysis of events and specific policies and legislation.

Part of the problem, as journalists themselves recognize, is that many members of the parliamentary press gallery have little or no background in politics and, moreover, often lack the highly developed skills required for detailed critical analysis.[69] Another part of the problem follows from the apparent apathy of the general public and many special interest groups concerning the legislative process in general and legislative issues in particular. It is our view that special efforts should be made by media interests to develop further their resources relative to Parliament. The benefits that would accrue to the public as well as to Parliament as a result of more thoroughgoing coverage and analysis would be considerable indeed.

The subject of broadcasting parliamentary proceedings is of particular interest to many parliamentarians. Most now approve the practice of broadcasting parliamentary proceedings begun in October, 1977, suggesting that Parliament is now "less remote" and "more relevant" and that both the Government and the Opposition now play their respective roles with greater care. They also contend that broadcasting has contributed to the improvement of accountability and hence to the strengthening of one of Parliament's central purposes. The live television coverage of the meetings of the Special Joint Committee on the Constitution gave ample proof of the importance and value of television coverage of Parliament's work, particularly its committees. For the first time many Canadians were able to watch their federal members in measured, thoughtful (yet still properly partisan) debate on an issue important to all Canadians rather than in the partisan hot-house atmosphere of question period. Increased television coverage of Parliament is an essential element of reform if increased accountability is to be achieved.

There are, of course, still problems to solve in connection with radio and television broadcasting in Parliament (particularly with respect to the privileges and immunities of members and witnesses). Nonetheless, most MPs seem to favour a partial extension of broadcasting to the standing committees. The only questions that are really unresolved are: to what extent will the standing committees be covered and what rules will apply? There is much resistance to the idea of covering all the standing committees, mostly because of cost. One suggestion is to equip one or two committee rooms fully and to schedule meetings in them that are of the greatest public interest.[70] This suggestion has merit and, in our view, should be examined carefully by the Special Committee on Standing Orders and Procedure.

It is our opinion that radio and television broadcasting of the activities of parliamentary committees would substantially benefit the parliamentary process. Accordingly, we recommend that:

34. Provisions be made within the House of Commons for the radio and television broadcasting of the activities of a limited number of standing committees and that the terms and conditions governing such coverage be determined by a special committee of the House.

As we have pointed out, changes in the legislative function are necessary if Parliament is to be in a position to respond to the challenges of the 1980s. Without change, Parliament as a forum for the debate of national issues and as a vital check on the power of the executive and public service, will continue to decline. To ensure that Canada has a healthy and responsive government, Parliament must regain its proper position as the primary institution of government.

SENATE REFORM AND REGIONAL REPRESENTATION

SINCE 1970, THE ISSUE OF parliamentary and senate reform has been joined by an even broader concern for the adequacy of regional representation in national institutions in general and in Parliament in particular. The entrenched regional basis of Canada's political parties, separatist sentiment in Quebec and western Canada, and a general sense of alienation from national institutions has fueled this growing concern. Several proposals for reform have emerged, including: a modified form of proportional representation in the House of Commons, a proposal for a House of Federation to replace the Senate as it is now constituted; and various proposals for an elected Senate. These proposals and their effects on the issues involved in reforming the House of Commons, the crucible of Parliament, warrant serious examination.

REGIONAL REPRESENTATION VERSUS THE "ONE PERSON—ONE VOTE"
The central question of Senate reform is whether regions, through some form of direct representation, should be given additional strength to act as a counterweight to the principle of one person-one vote, on which the House of Commons is elected.

The House of Commons does, of course, represent regions in that members of Parliament are elected from geographically defined constituencies across Canada. These constituencies are not drawn purely on a "rep-by-pop" basis, in that consideration is also given to factors that marginally reward rural constituencies over urban ones. Moreover, there is always a lag in actual representation since the redefinition of constituency boundaries occurs long after census data are taken. Unquestionably, regional voices are present in the House of Commons and regional "representation" is present. It is, however, because of party discipline, given expression behind the scenes in caucus and cabinet.

But the essential question is whether this "representation" leads to the exercise of regional *power*—that is, does the decision-making process that results act in a way that is sensitive to the main concerns of the regions of Canada? The criteria for sufficiency cannot be absolute. All regions cannot, by definition, have their way all the time. Nor can they be allowed to produce a perpetual series of stalemates with the national decision-making process immobilized by an unworkable "double majority". In short, representation by population cannot be stalemated through representation by region. The adequacy of regional representation and regional power, however, is always itself an act of evolving political and democratic judgment.

The Senate has been the main federal institution where a form of representation by region or district had been constitutionally recognized. The *British North America Act* initially provided for a Senate composed of three divisions. These were increased to four in 1915. Each division was entitled to equal representation by 24 Senators appointed by the Governor in Council. Newfoundland and the two Territories were also given Senators.

However useful the Senate has been as a body of "sober second thought" in the legislative process, it is generally agreed that it does not function as a viable forum of regional representation. Its first defect is that the basis of its composition, despite its regional format, *reinforces* representation by population. The two largest provinces, Ontario and Quebec have 46% of the Senate seats as well as 60% of the House of Commons. As the study on regional representation undertaken by the Canada West Foundation in 1981 correctly points out, "Canada is the only democratic federal system in the world in which the regions with the largest populations dominate both houses of the national legislature".[71] This inadequacy is compounded by the fact that Senators are not elected; they are appointed on the basis of political patronage with little, if any, consultation with provincial leaders. Moreover, the "districts" they "represent"—and this is especially so for Senators from Western Canada and the Maritimes—are too diffuse for practical political representation.

There can be little doubt that provinces offer the most practical and recognized boundaries by which to define a political region in Canada for purposes of Senate representation.

The need for representation by region as distinct from representation by population has been recognized and accommodated in many different ways in Canada's political institutions. The most obvious way is through federalism itself, a system of governing based on separate defined spheres of government power. The evolution of federalism in Canada testifies also to the need for cooperation and collaboration between the federal government and Canada's "regional" constituent units, the provinces. On the other hand, the failure to secure adequate regional representation through national institutions has resulted in virtually all regional views being identified with provincial governments and their premiers. This has been especially noticeable since 1970.

The failure of national institutions in Canada to reflect and to respond adequately to regional concerns is not purely the result of failure by successive federal governments. The simple plurality (first-past-the-post) electoral system skews electoral results in significant ways. Today, this is particularly reflected in the "under-representation" of Progressive Conservatives in Quebec and of Liberals in Western Canada. This means that the Parliamentary caucuses of the national political parties are seriously out of balance in regional terms and that important voices, therefore, go unheard in crucial day-to-day politics. The parties also have difficulty conducting national campaigns and fear the loss of their largely regional bases of support. When cabinets are formed (primarily Liberal cabinets) there has been a corresponding weakness in regional cabinet representation. And on, and on, the political spiral goes. Regional weakness begets more regional weakness and national institutions become deservedly suspect.

These considerations are reinforced by two other realities that make a concern for regionalism a political imperative in Canada. These are: the possibility of separatism; and, the pervasive strength of regional views despite the influence of mass communications—which should ordinarily exercise a homogenizing influence on the attitudes of Canadians. The key difference between disenchanted groups that are regionally or territorially based and those that are nationally based, such as "the poor" or "the middle class", is that the former can contemplate separation. The concerns of French Canadians are real not just because they are a linguistic minority in an anglophone continent, but also because they are concentrated territorially in one region. The concerns of Western Canadians can be and are couched in separatist terms as well. In short, the issue of the representativeness of regions and political power in national institutions deserves attention because separatism is no longer a mere theoretical option.

In addition to separatism there are other deep underlying social attitudes which have contributed to the growth of regionalism. Modern industrialization, mass communications, and consumer marketing trends have all exerted influences on the Canadian population which should tend to make it homogeneous. And yet regionalism has never been stronger. It challenges these pressures toward assimilation. Citing recent studies on this phenomenon, the Canada West Foundation attributes this paradox of "objective homogeneity" coexisting with increasing "subjective regionalism", to the rise of the individual and individualism. The latter "requires decentralization, small scale organizations, and consensus (rather than simple majoritarianism) for its greatest realization".

All of the preceding factors argue a compelling case for the need to reform the regional basis of representation in Canada's national institutions. In a sense, in 1979 and 1980, Canada's political leaders each addressed half of the Canadian dilemma. Prime Minister Trudeau asked "Who speaks for Canada?" and former Prime Minister Clark espoused a view of Canada as a "community of communities". Both inherently recognize the need to reform the forum for regional representation at the centre. The question is what kind of reforms are workable and acceptable?

MAJOR REFORM IDEAS

There have been numerous proposals for reform related directly or indirectly to the issue of regional representation but three ideas in particular stand out. The first, is a modified form of proportional representation which deals with the House of Commons itself. The other two involve Senate reform, one proposing to alter the basis of appointment (through indirect election) and the second recommending establishment of an elected Senate.

The idea of a modified system of proportional voting is intended to overcome the under-representation of party strength in Canada's regions. The idea is to elect an *additional* set of members of Parliament from each province or region selected in any one of a number of possible ways (e.g. a party list, or the selection of several second place finishers) to obtain representation in Ottawa that more accurately reflects the distribution of the popular vote in each defined region. The caucus of each party would then contain a more representative mix of regional voices.

Such a system would produce a larger House of Commons, and could conceivably be criticized for creating a group of "second class" members of Parliament. However, the most fundamental objection is that it would be precisely what it is—a marginal and episodic "add on" to whatever the electoral results produce. Since no modified electoral system is likely to be accepted if it reduces the prospect for majority government, the additional members of Parliament would not fundamentally alter the current reality. Moreover, such a system would add a further (unnecessary) burden to the House of Commons whose task of representing Canadians "by population" is already sufficiently difficult (even with the benefit of the reforms proposed in this study).

There are strong reasons to focus regional representation in a reformed Senate. In addition to its "sober second thought" and overall legislative review functions, this is the usual and accepted role for an "upper house" in other federal systems.

The Government of Canada's *Constitutional Amendment Bill* introduced in 1978 (Bill C-60) has, to date, been the most concrete proposal for a more representative Senate. It proposed a new upper house to be called the House of Federation. The allocation of members to the new upper house was to have a provincial basis but with no obvious rationale. Equal representation by province was rejected. The Ontario and Quebec portion of seats was to be reduced and Western Canadian seats significantly increased.

Fifty-nine members (half of the total of 118 members) would represent the provincial political parties in proportion to each party's share of the popular vote in the most recent *provincial* election. The other half would represent national political parties on a similar basis relative to federal elections. Thus there would be a form of revolving door membership as electoral fates changed.

Federal thinking envisioned reduced and more focussed powers for the new upper house compared to those possessed by the existing Senate. It could not originate money bills. The House of Federation could delay legislation for 60 to 120 days but the House of Commons could overcome this with a two-thirds vote on urgent matters. Proposed in the wake of the election of a separatist Parti Québecois Government in Quebec, the federal initiative would also give the upper house powers over "measures of special linguistic significance", requiring a double majority of French and English-speaking members of the new House of Federation. This could only be overturned by the House of Commons with an unusual majority vote. The new House of Federation would also have the power to ratify federal nominations to the Supreme Court and nominations for ambassadors and heads of some agencies and Crown corporations.

The proposal for a House of Federation has a mixture of strengths and weaknesses. Certainly, it would increase regional representation but its focus is clearly on linguistic issues. The general power to delay is really only a power to publicize. It overcomes only part of the problem of the narrow regional base of Canada's political parties. Regional views would be broadened and would not necessarily be the views only of the provincial governments. Members would be only indirectly elected and so accountability would be only vaguely established. The hodge-podge nature of the House of Federation and its powers would make it difficult to create a coherent legislative body, especially if the power to delay is its only real power in relation to general legislative matters.

The most comprehensive proposal for a full-fledged elected Senate comes from a previously-mentioned task force sponsored by the Canada West Foundation. The task force argues that an *elected* Senate based on equal representation for each province is the best way to secure practical and focussed accountability for regional concerns. Non-elected representatives lack "a firm popular and constitutional basis for their influence".[72] This is the basis for other systems such as in Australia, the United States, and Switzerland—countries with regional dilemmas approaching those of Canada. The Canada West Foundation's task force recommended that Senators be elected at large on the basis of a single province-wide constituency. Elections for Senators would also coincide with national general elections and the sitting term of a Senate would coincide with the life of a Parliament. However, the elected term for a Senator would be over *two* Parliaments. Consequently, only half of the Senators of any province would be elected at any one national general election.

We are strongly persuaded that the current inadequacies of regional representation and power through national institutions are serious and constitute a major threat to Canada's political, economic and social future. We believe that major change is necessary. Accordingly, we recommend that:

35. **The Senate of Canada be elected on the basis of equal representation for each province and that it be given the necessary powers to reflect the regional concerns of Canada while maintaining the House of Commons as the primary forum for majoritarian and responsible parliamentary government.**

An elected Senate would complement the House of Commons and the reforms we have proposed.

IMPLICATIONS OF AN ELECTED SENATE

In general, we are convinced that the reforms proposed elsewhere in this study will enhance both responsible parliamentary government and the regional sensitivity of the House of Commons. The elected Senate, however, would be the primary regional forum in Canada's Parliament. It must have suitable powers to reflect regional concerns but not the overall power to immobilize majoritarian government.

The issue of "confidence" and political party discipline in the elected Senate can perhaps be resolved. The government should be required to command the confidence of the House of Commons only. There should be no requirement for the government to resign or call an election merely because a vote is lost in the elected Senate. The Senate should also function on the basis of free votes. The House of Commons is a place of partisanship and party discipline and the focal point for confidence. The elected Senate should not become a duplicate institution but rather one that freely reflects regional concerns and seeks to help resolve them.

Two further issues follow from the above. The Senate should not have the power to initiate money bills but should, as it does now and as we have suggested earlier in this study, have a role in scrutinizing public taxing and spending decisions. Moreover, Senators should not be permitted to become cabinet ministers unless they resign from the Senate and secure an elected seat in the Commons at the next election or at an early electoral opportunity.

As proposed by the federal government in 1978, the Senate should also have the power to ratify appointments to the Supreme Court of Canada and to designated federal boards, agencies and corporations. These would be the key powers. In all other respects the Senate would retain its role in the legislative process. There would, however, have to be an "override" voting rule by which the House of Commons could, with an extraordinary majority (e.g. 60 per cent) pass legislation defeated or unduly delayed in the Senate.

There are, of course, other powers which could be considered, but these need not concern us here. The point to be stressed is that an elected Senate can help address a serious problem in the representativeness of Canada's national institutions provided that its links to majoritarian and responsible parliamentary government are carefully considered and respected. A reformed House of Commons and an elected Senate will help produce the effective and accountable government which Canadians have every right to expect and which present national institutions are ill-equipped to provide.

Afterword

The recommendations put forward in this study are advanced in the belief that reform of Canada's parliamentary institutions is necessary if our system of government is to meet the growing demands of our modern society, and if Parliament is to regain the respect and trust of the electorate. However, change, in the context of any fundamental institution of society must be approached with caution and due regard to its impact. The approach to reform must be deliberate, gradual, informed and responsible.

We have attempted to report faithfully upon the frustration and impatience that parliamentarians experience when faced with the obvious need for change and the slow rate of progress to date. However, Parliament *is* responding and significant work *is* underway. As related earlier in this study, the House of Commons Special Committee on Standing Orders and Procedure has already carried out a comprehensive analysis of some of the major issues outstanding. The provisional changes that have been made to the Standing Orders of the House of Commons will, in time, improve the internal effectiveness of the business of governing the country. But this is only a beginning. Additional reform recommendations are expected from the Special Committee and should command the attention and scrutiny of all those who wish to particpate in the debate on parliamentary reform. Also, a Special Joint Committee of the Senate and the House of Commons has been struck to study reform of the Senate. This Special Joint Committee will commence hearings in 1983 and will no doubt enunciate major reform proposals.

An appreciation of the work of these committees by those outside Parliament will lead to a better informed commentary on parliamentary reform and, most importantly, will raise the political profile and importance of the parliamentary reform issue in Canada. Only if Canadians demand reform of their parliamentary institutions will the necessary political will be mustered. The approach should be non-partisan and draw upon the expertise, historical knowledge and wisdom found in the provincial legislatures as well as in government and opposition parties in the House of Commons and the Senate.

The authors hope this study will have an educational application and that it will bring home to those of us who are not continuing students of government the importance of the means we choose to order our society. The institutions and mechanisms of government must be recognized as *fundamental* institutions—so pervasive that all segments and sectors of society must relate to them, be subordinate to them, and be compatible with them—as we go about deciding what form Canadian society will take. Business people and labour leaders must join with politicians and officials to search for, document, and implement the systems of governance that will work in contemporary Canada.

Analysis, thinking and decision-making about these matters should not be limited to senior individuals and officials only. Managers at all levels, foremen, teachers, students and workers should all be aware of the forces at play, the strategies of reform and the realities that trigger political motivation. Without such knowledge, any public debate will be meaningless, if there is any debate at all. Without informed debate on parliamentary reform, decision-making will—dangerously—be the sole preserve of politicians. Politicians may well be most knowledgeable of the internal workings of Parliament and the areas and issues most in need of reform but, by themselves, they are unlikely to identify and correct the perceptions of many Canadians—that Parliament is an inconsequential centre of national debate and leadership. Such a sense of urgency and meaningful reform can only come from a broadly-based consensus of Canadians from all walks of life.

Most Canadians would opt for measures that would transform Parliament from its present status and capabilities into a new crucible for national dialogue and leadership. The time for action is upon us.

RECOMMENDATIONS

OUR RECOMMENDATIONS have been extracted from the text and are set out below with their page references.

We recommend that:

1. The leaders of both the government and opposition parties recognize and adopt in practice a less stringent approach to the question of party discipline and the rules governing confidence. *Page 30*

2. Where a minimum of 50 members of Parliament (at least 10 of whom are drawn from each of two political parties) agree that a subject warrants committee investigation, a committee for such a purpose shall be created, or an existing committee shall be assigned to investigate the subject. Only two such new committees should co-exist at any time during any session of Parliament. *Page 32*

3. Standing committees be given the power to select subjects within their jurisdiction for investigation. *Page 32*

4. A new doctrine of deputy ministerial responsibility to Parliament be established relating exclusively to matters of administration. The doctrine would set out the obligations of senior public servants and would include the obligation to testify before parliamentary committees on matters of administration. *Page 45*

5. The principle of public service neutrality be re-affirmed as the guiding factor in all senior appointments whether filled from within or from outside the public service. *Page 48*

111

6. Appointments at the deputy and assistant-deputy minister level be made with a view towards increasing the number of qualified non-career public servants in such positions. *Page 50*

7. Ministers be encouraged to appoint personal policy advisers who will hold their appointments at the pleasure of the minister. *Page 51*

8. A full senior-junior ministry system be adopted that maintains a satisfactory regional representation in the senior ministry. *Page 51*

9. More explanatory materials accompany the budget papers submitted to Parliament by the minister of finance. *Page 64*

10. The minister of finance be required to publish with the budget additional data on tax expenditures showing in detail the connection, by program, between the tax expenditures and major direct expenditures in each program area. *Page 66*

11. A standing committee of the House of Commons be established to investigate and scrutinize the finances of selected crown corporations each year. *Page 70*

12. The minister of finance and the president of the treasury board be required jointly to publish an annual white paper on government expenditure. Such a document should contain information on expenditure plans and projections over a three- to five-year period, on a departmental and program basis as well as on the basis of economic category of expenditure. The document should also include a projection of revenues for the same time period and information on the government's medium-term economic forecast and the assumptions underlying it. *Page 71*

13. The white paper on government expenditure be presented to Parliament late in each calendar year (prior to the presentation of the blue book estimates) and that a one-day parliamentary debate follow that presentation. *Page 71*

14. A new standing committee on the expenditure budget be established to receive and scrutinize the white paper and to invite testimony on its contents. *Page 71*

15. Four departments and agencies—two selected by the opposi-

tion parties and two by the government—each year be required to submit to Parliament a departmental "green book" evaluation of its programs, such evaluations to be tabled at the same time as the estimates blue book. *Page 71*

16. A joint House of Commons-Senate committee on economic policy be created and that it be co-chaired by a government member and an opposition member. The committee's task should be: to hold pre-budget hearings; to receive testimony from the minister of finance, the president of the treasury board, and the governor of the Bank of Canada; to receive and scrutinize the annual reviews of the Economic Council of Canada; and to hear testimony from such non-governmental experts and organizations as required. *Page 76*

17. A subcommittee of the House of Commons standing committee on finance, trade and economic affairs be established to conduct an ongoing review of major changes in tax policy. *Page 76*

18. Members allow the structural and technical provisions in a tax bill to be separated from the bill during the legislative process and scrutinized by an appropriate parliamentary committee. *Page 76*

19. Fifteen private members' public bills be allowed to come to a vote in the House each session. *Page 81*

20. The staff budget for a member's Ottawa office be increased to allow a member, at his discretion, to hire one additional assistant to aid him in carrying out his legislative responsibilities. *Page 83*

21. The government permit individual members to play a greater role in policy formulation by more frequently preparing and referring to committees white papers and green papers on major areas of public policy. *Page 86*

22. Parliament experiment actively with the referral of bills to committee without debate after first reading. *Page 86*

23. In order to facilitate recommendation 22, the government be required to produce a major portion of its legislative program, including draft bills, early in the debate on the Address in Reply to the speech from the throne. *Page 86*

24. The House leaders routinely attempt to reach agreement on distinguishing major bills from minor bills, and that major bills be sent to committee after first reading. *Page 87*

25. Committee chairmen be elected on the basis of their leadership skills (not because of their loyalty to the government) by a simple majority vote of the committee members. *Page 89*

26. Chairmen be routinely re-elected as long as they continue to provide satisfactory leadership. *Page 89*

27. To make the position of committee chairman as attractive to a member of parliament as the position of parliamentary secretary now is, similar remuneration should be attached to both positions. *Page 89*

28. A study of the likely staff requirements of a strengthened committee system be undertaken as soon as possible. *Page 90*

29. The House of Commons sit for a maximum of 150 days a year, plus the number of days needed for committee work. *Page 91*

30. Parliamentary sessions operate on the basis of five-week cycles, each cycle consisting of three weeks of regular sittings, followed by one week of committee hearings and one week of adjournment to permit members to carry out their constituency work. *Page 91*

31. The draft regulations (delegated legislation) contemplated for a new bill accompany the new bill when it is presented to Parliament, thus permitting the joint committee on regulations and other statutory instruments to comment on the draft legislation. *Page 97*

32. The provisions of draft legislation granting regulation-making powers should automatically be referred upon second reading to the standing joint committee on regulations and other statutory instruments for study and comment. *Page 97*

33. The distinction between "regulations" and "statutory instruments" be removed from the *Statutory Instruments Act* to enable a more complete scrutiny of all subordinate rule making by Parliament. *Page 97*

34. Provisions be made within the House of Commons for the

radio and television broadcasting of the activities of a limited number of standing committees and that the terms and conditions governing such coverage be determined by a special committee of the House. *Page 99*

35. The Senate of Canada be elected on the basis of equal representation for each province and that it be given the necessary powers to reflect the regional concerns of Canada while maintaining the House of Commons as the primary forum for majoritarian and responsible parliamentary government. *Page 107*

CITATIONS

1. Kenneth Kernaghan, "Politics, Policy and Public Servants: Political Neutrality Revisited", *Canadian Public Administration*, Vol. 19, No. 3 (Spring 1977) p. 432.
2. John B. Stewart, *The Canadian House of Commons* (Montreal and London; McGill-Queen's University Press, 1977), p. 14.
3. *Ibid.* p. 15.
4. *Ibid.* p. 97.
5. Peter Self. *Administrative Theories and Policies* (London: George Allen and Unwin, 1972), p. 290.
6. Michael J. Crozier, Samuel P. Huntington, and Joji Watanuki, *The Crisis of Democracy* (New York: New York University Press, 1975), pp. 163 and 164.
7. "The Present State of the Legislative Process in Canada: Myths and Realities", a paper presented to the Conference on the Future of the Legislative Process, Victoria, (March 31, 1978) and published in William A. Neilson and James C. MacPherson, eds., *The Legislative Process in Canada: The Need for Reform* (Montreal: Institute for Research on Public Policy, 1978).
8. Thomas d'Aquino, "The Prime Minister's Office: Catalyst or Cabal? Aspects of the Development of the Office and Some Thoughts about its Future", *Canadian Public Administration*, Vol. 17, No. 1 (Spring 1974).
9. Marc Lalonde, "The Changing Role of the Prime Minister's Office", a paper presented to the 23rd Annual Meeting of the Institute of Public Administration of Canada (September 8, 1971).
10. Colin Campbell, and George J. Szablowski, *The Super-Bureaucrats* (Toronto: Macmillan of Canada, 1979), p. 2.
11. House of Commons Debates, (Tuesday, December 5, 1978), Vol. 122, No 40, 4th Session, 30th Parliament, pp. 1811-1815.
12. Third Report of the Special Committee on Standing Orders and Procedures, in *Votes and Proceedings of the House of Commons* for Friday, November 5, 1982 (Hull: Canadian Government Publishing Centre), p.5.

13. "Federalism and the Legislative Process in Canada", a paper presented to the Conference on the Future of the Legislative Process, Victoria, (March 31, 1978) and published in William A. Neilson and James C. MacPherson, eds., *The Legislative Process in Canada: The Need for Reform* (Montreal: Institute for Research on Public Policy, 1978).

14. Denis Smith, "President and Parliament: The Transformation of Parliamentary Government in Canada", Thomas A. Hockin, ed., *Apex of Power* (Toronto: McGraw-Hill Ryerson, 1971). p. 224.

15. J. R. Mallory, "Responsive and Responsible Government". Transactions of the Royal Society of Canada, Series IV, Vol. XII (1974).

16. H. V. Emy, "The Public Service and Political Control: The Problem of Accountability in a Westminster System with Special Reference to the Concept of Ministerial Responsibility", a study prepared for the Coombes Commission, Austraila (1977). p. 19.

17. Kenneth Kernaghan, "Power, Parliament and Public Servants in Canada: Ministerial Responsibility Reexamined", a paper prepared for the Conference on Legislative Studies in Canada, Simon Fraser University, (February 15-17, 1979). p. 1.

18. *Ibid*, pp. 3 and 4.

19. Select Committee on Procedure, 1977-78 Session *First Report* (London: Her Majesty's Stationery Office, 1978).

20. Emy, The Public Service and Political Control, *op. cit.* p. 21.

21. John B. Stewart, *The Canadian House of Commons* (Montreal and London: McGill-Queen's University Press, 1977). p. 84.

22. Hon. Richard J. Stanbury, Q.C., *Liberal Party of Canada—An Interpretation* (Ottawa: The Liberal Party of Canada, 1969).

23. Richard D. French, "Freedom of Information and Parliament", a paper prepared for The Conference on Legislative Studies in Canada, Simon Fraser University, Vancouver (Feb. 15-17, 1979). Also, Hon. John Roberts P.C., M.P., Notes for an address to the National Conference on Freedom of Information, University of Victoria (March 23, 1979).

24. David Zussman, "The Image of the Public Service in Canada", *Canadian Public Administration*, Vol. 25, No. 1 (Spring 1982) pp. 72-73.

25. *The Globe and Mail*, July 15, 1982, p. 1.

26. Flora MacDonald, in a speech to the Canadian Political Science Association, Annual Meeting, University of Quebec, June 3, 1980; rewritten and published in P. W. Fox, ed., *Politics Canada*, 5th Edition (Toronto: McGraw-Hill Ryerson, 1982) pp. 471-476.

27. G. Bruce Doern and Richard M. Phidd, *Ottawa's Decisions: Canadian Public Policy* (Toronto: Methuen, 1983), Chapter 10.

28. Senator P. M. Pitfield, in a speech to the Ottawa Kiwanis Club, February 25, 1983.

29. Rt. Hon. Joe Clark, P.C., M.P., in a speech to the Victoria Chamber of Commerce, Victoria, B.C., February 28, 1983.

30. *Ottawa Citizen*, January 5, 1979.
31. Thomas d'Aquino, *The Minister's Office—A Study in Aid of Ministerial Decision-Making* (Ottawa: Office of the Prime Minister, 1970).
32. Blair Williams, "The Para-Political Bureacuracy in Ottawa", a paper prepared for the Conference on Legislative Studies in Canada, Simon Fraser University, Vancouver (February 15-17, 1979). p. 23.
33. Hal V. Kroeker, *Accountability and Control of the Government Expenditure Process* (Montreal: C. D. Howe Research Institute, 1978). p. 31.
34. G. Bruce Doern and Allen Maslove, eds., *The Public Evaluation of Government Spending* (Montreal: Institute for Research on Public Policy, 1979), Chapter 1.
35. Treasury Board, *Policy and Expenditure Management System: Envelope Procedures and Rules*, July 1981, pp. 1-2.
36. G. Bruce Doern, ed., *How Ottawa Spends Your Tax Dollars 1981* (Toronto: Lorimer, 1981), chapter 1.
37. See R. Van Loon, "Ottawa's Envelopes: Four Systems in Search of Co-ordination" in G. B. Doern, ed., *How Ottawa Spends—1983* (Toronto: Lorimer, 1983), chapter 4.
38. Kroeker, *Accountability and Control, op cit*, pp. 37-38 and Douglas Hartle, *The Expenditure Budget Process in Canada* (Toronto: Canadian Tax Foundation, 1978). pp. 34-36.
39. David Good, *The Politics of Anticipation: Making Canadian Federal Tax Policy* (Ottawa: School of Public Administration, Carleton University, 1980).
40. Canadian Tax Foundation, "The Tax Legislative Process", A Report to the Honourable Jean Chretien, Minister of Finance (November, 1977).
41. Paul Thomas, "Parliament and the Purse Strings", a study prepared for the Royal Commission on Financial Management and Accountability (Ottawa: 1977) and P. C. Dobell, "Parliament and the Control of Public Expenditure", a Report to the Royal Commission on Financial Management and Accountability (Ottawa: 1977).
42. House of Commons Debates, (Tuesday, December 5, 1978), Vol. 122, No. 40, 4th Session, 30th Parliament, p. 1813.
43. Allan Maslove, "Tax Expenditures: The Other Side of Government Spending", a paper presented to the Conference on Forums and Methods for Public Evaluation of Government Spending, Ottawa, (October 20, 1978).
44. David Good, *The Politics of Anticipation: Making Canadian Federal Tax Policy op. cit.*
45. Allan Tupper and G. Bruce Doren, eds., *Public Corporations and Public Policy in Canada* (Montreal: Institute for Research on Public Policy, 1981).
46. Douglas Hartle, "Canada's Watchdog Growing Too Strong?", *The Globe and Mail*, January 10, 1979. p. 7.

47. Canada, *The Budget Process* (Ottawa: Department of Finance, April, 1982).
48. Canadian Tax Foundation, "The Tax Legislative Process" submitted to then Finance Minister Chretien in November, 1977 and subsequently published in *The Canadian Tax Journal*, Vol. xxvi, March/April 1978, pp. 157-182.
49. *Ibid.* p. vii.
50. *Ibid.* p. v.
51. *Ibid.* p. vii.
52. Audrey Doerr, "The Role of White Papers" in G. Bruce Doern and Peter Aucoin, eds., *The Structures of Policy Making in Canada* (Toronto: Macmillan, 1971). Chapter 6.
53. Hon. Ronald Huntington, P.C., M.P. and Claude-Andre Lachance, M.P., "Accountability: Closing the Loop", a paper submitted to the Special Committee of the House of Commons on Standing Orders and Procedure, (November 8, 1982). p. 24.
54. Stewart, *The Canadian House of Commons op. cit*, pp. 6-7.
55. Mark MacGuigan, P.C., M.P., "Parliamentary Reform: Impediments to an Enlarged Role for the Backbencher", *Legislative Studies Quarterly*, Vol. III, No. 4 (November, 1978). p. 677.
56. Stewart, *The Canadian House of Commons, op. cit.* p. 73.
57. MacGuigan, "Parliamentary Reform: Impediments to an Enlarged Role for the Backbencher". *op. cit.*
58. Alistair Fraser, "Legislators and their Staffs", a paper prepared for the Legislative Studies in Canada Conference, Simon Fraser University, Vancouver, (February 15-17, 1979). p. 15.
59. Hartle, "Canada's Watchdog Growing Too Strong?", *op. cit.*
60. Peter C. Dobell, "Committee Staff—What Else is Needed?", a paper prepared for the Conference on Legislative Studies in Canada, Simon Fraser University, Vancouver, (February 15-17, 1979). pp. 9-12.
61. Third Report of the Special Committee on Standing Orders and Procedure, published in *Votes and Proceedings of the House of Commons* for Friday, November 5, 1982 (Hull: Canadian Government Publishing Centre), p. 14.
62. Michel Arneller, ed., *Parliaments. A Comparative Study on the Structure and Functioning of Representative Institutions in Fifty-five Countries* (London: Cassels, 1966). p. 152.
63. *Statutory Instruments Acts*, s.c. 1970-71-72, c. 38, Section 1 (1) (d).
64. *Responsible Regulation* (Ottawa: Economic Council of Canada, 1980).
65. Bill C-33. Third Session. 30th Parliament (April 6, 1978).
66. G. Bruce Doern and Richard W. Phidd, *Ottawa's Decisions: Canadian Public Policy op. cit.*, chapters 13 and 14.
67. William H. R. Charles, "Public Policy and Legislative Drafting", a paper presented to the Conference on the Future of the Legislative Process, Victoria (March 31, 1978), and published in William A. Neilson and

James C. MacPherson, eds., *The Legislative Process in Canada: The Need for Reform* (Montreal: Institute for Research on Public Policy, 1978).

68. *Regulation Reference, A Report to the First Ministers* (Ottawa: Economic Council of Canada, 1978).

69. Geoffrey Stevens, "The Influence and Responsibilities of the Media in the Legislative Process", a paper presented to the Conference on the Future of the Legislative Process, Victoria (March 31, 1978), and published in William A. Neilson and J. C. MacPherson, eds., *The Legislative Process in Canada*. Institute for Research on Public Policy. (Toronto: Butterworth, 1978). p. 228.

70. Gordon Cullingham, "Broadcasting the House of Commons", a paper prepared for the Conference on Legislative Studies in Canada, Simon Fraser University, Vancouver (February 15-17, 1979).

71. *Regional Representation, The Canadian Partnership* (Calgary: Canada West Foundation, 1981) p. 29.

72. *Ibid.* p. 109.

BIBLIOGRAPHY

Anderson, J.E. "Pressure Groups and the Canadian Bureaucracy", in Kenneth Kernaghan, ed., *Public Administration in Canada: Selected Readings*, 3rd ed. (Toronto: Methuen. 1977).

Arneller, Michael, ed. *Parliaments. A Comparative Study on the Structure and Functioning of Representative Institutions in Fifty-five Countries* (London: Cassels, 1966).

Birch, A.H. *Representative and Responsible Government*, (London: George Allen and Unwin, 1964).

Bird, Richard M. and David K. Foot "Bureaucratic Growth in Canada: Myths and Realities", paper for the Conference on Public Evaluation of Government Spending, Carleton University, Ottawa (October 20, 1978).

Black, Edwin R. "Opposition Research: Some Theories and Practice", *Canadian Public Administration*, Vol. XV No. 1, (Spring 1972).

Blair, Ronald "What Happens to Parliament?", in Trevor Lloyd and Jack MacLeod, eds., *Agenda 1970*, (Toronto: University of Toronto Press, 1968).

Brooke, Jeffrey *A Comparison of the Role of the Minister's Office in France, Britain and Canada*, (Ottawa: Library of Parliament, Research Branch, 1978).

Campbell, Colin and George J. Szablowski *The Superbureaucrats: Structure & Behaviour in Central Agencies* (Toronto: Macmillan of Canada, 1979).

Canada West Foundation *Regional Representation, the Canadian Partnership* (Calgary, 1981).

Canadian Tax Foundation "The Tax Legislative Process," A report to the Honourable Jean Chrétien, Minister of Finance (November 1977).

Charles, William H.R. "Public Policy and Legislative Drafting", eds., W.A.W. Neilson and J.C. MacPherson, *The Legislative Process in Canada: The Need for Reform* (Montreal: Institute for Research on Public Policy, 1978).

Clarke, Harold and Colin Campbell, F.G. and Arthur Goddard *Parliament Policy and Representation* (Toronto: Methuen 1980).

Crick, Bernard *The Reform of Parliament,* 2nd ed. (London: Weidenfeld & Nicholson, 1968).

Crossman, R.H.S. "Canadian Issues As Seen From Outside", in Gordon Hawkins, ed., *Order and Good Government* (Toronto: Canadian Institute of Public Affairs, 1965).

Crossman, Richard *The Diaries of a Cabinet Minister,* Vol. 1, 2, and 3 (London: Hamish Hamilton and J. Cape, 1975, 1976, and 1977).

Crozier, Michael J., Samuel P. Huntington and J. Watanuki *The Crisis of Democracy* (New York: New York University Press, 1975).

Cullingham, Gordon "Broadcasting the House of Commons", a paper prepared for the Conference on Legislative Studies in Canada, Simon Fraser University, Vancouver (February 15-17, 1979).

d'Aquino, Thomas *The Minister's Office—A Study in Aid of Ministerial Decision-Making* (Ottawa: Office of the Prime Minister, 1970).

_____ "The Prime Minister's Office: Catalyst or Cabal? Aspects of the Development of the Office and Some Thoughts About its Future.", *Canadian Public Administration,* Vol. 17, No. 1 (Spring 1974).

Dawson, W.F. *Procedure in the Canadian House of Commons* (Toronto: University of Toronto Press, 1962).

Dawson, R. and W.F. Dawson *Democratic Government in Canada,* 4th ed. Rev. by Norman Ward (Toronto: University of Toronto Press, 1971).

Dobell, Rodney and David Zussman "An Evaluation System for Government: If Politics is Theatre, then Evaluation is (Mostly) Art", *Canadian Public Administration:* Vol. 24, No. 3, pp. 404-427 (Fall 1981).

Dobell, P.C. "Parliament and the Control of Public Expenditure", Report to the Royal Commission on Financial Management and Accountability, Ottawa (1977).

_____ **and Susan d'Aquino** "The Special Joint Committee on Immigration Policy 1975: An Exercise in Participatory Democracy", Canadian Institute on International Affairs, Behind the Headlines, (1976).

_____ "Committee Staff—What Else is Needed?" A paper prepared for the Second Legislative Studies in Canada Conference, Simon Fraser University, Vancouver, B.C. (February 1979).

Doern, G. Bruce, ed. *The Regulatory Process in Canada* (Toronto: Macmillan of Canada, 1978).

_____ "Public Scrutiny of Canadian Government Spending, the Case for an Annual White Paper on Government Expenditure", Rideau Public Policy Research Group, Ottawa (1978).

_____ The Relevance and Transferability of Selected British Institutions of Financial Accountability to Canada", Report prepared for the Royal Commission on Financial Management and Accountability, Ottawa (1977).

_____ *How Ottawa Spends your Tax Dollars: National Policy and Economic Development 1982* (Toronto: James Lorimer, 1982).

_____ *How Ottawa Spends—1983* (Toronto: James Lorimer, 1983).

_____ **and Peter Aucoin, eds.** *Canadian Public Policy: Organization Process and Management* (Toronto: Macmillan of Canada, 1979).

_____ **and Peter C. Aucoin** *The Structures of Policy Making in Canada* (Toronto: Macmillan of Canada, 1971).

_____ **and Richard W. Phidd** *Ottawa's Decisions: Canadian Public Policy Ideas, Structures and Process* (Toronto: Methuen 1973).

_____ **and Allan Maslove, ed.** *The Public Evaluation of Government Spending* (Montreal: Institute for Research on Public Policy, 1979).

Doerr, Audrey "The Role of White Papers" in Doern and Aucoin, *The Structures of Policy Making in Canada* (Toronto: Macmillan of Canada, 1971).

Economic Council of Canada *Regulation Reference, A Report to First Ministers* (Ottawa: Ministry of Supply and Services, 1978).

_____ *Responsible Regulation,* (Ottawa: Ministry of Supply and Services, 1980).

Else, Peter *The Power of the Purse: The Role of European Parliaments in Budgetary Decisions* (London: George Allen & Unwin, 1976).

Emy, H.V. "The Public Service and Political Control: The Problem of Accountability in a Westminster System with Special Reference to the Concept of Ministerial Responsibility," a study prepared for the Coombes Commission, Australia (1977).

Flemming, Brian "The Prime Minister's Office: A Functional Source of Political Advice", *Hearsay,* Dalhousie University Law School, (August 1978).

_____ *Responsible Regulation* (Ottawa: Ministry of Supply and Services, 1979).

Franks, C.E.S. "The Reform of Parliament", *Queen's Quarterly* (Spring 1969).

_____ "The Committee Clerks of the Canadian House of Commons", *The Parliamentarian,* No. 50 (1969).

_____ "The Dilemma of the Standing committees of the Canadian House of Commons", *Canadian Journal of Political Science,* Vol. IV, (December 1971).

_____ "Procedural Reform in the Legislative Process", eds., W.A.W. Neilson and J.C. MacPherson, *The Legislative Process in Canada: The Need for Reform,* (Montreal: Institute for Research on Public Policy, 1978).

Fraser, John A., M.P. a comment on "The Backbencher and The Discharge of Legislative Responsibilities", by John Reid, M.P., in W.A.W. Neilson and J.C. MacPherson, eds., *The Legislative Process in Canada: The Need for Reform,* (Montreal: Institute for Research on Public Policy, 1978).

Fraser, Alistair "Legislators and their Staffs", a paper prepared for the

Conference on Legislative Studies in Canada, Simon Fraser University, Vancouver, (February, 1979).

French, Richard D. *How Ottawa Decides* (Toronto: Lorimer, 1980).

_____ "The Privy Council Office: Support for Cabinet Decision Making", in Richard Schultz et al *The Canadian Political Process*, 3rd Edition (Toronto: Holt, Rinehart and Winston, 1970).

_____ "Freedom of Information and Parliament", a paper prepared for the Conference on Legislative Studies in Canada, Simon Fraser University, Vancouver (February 15-17, 1979).

Fox, Paul W. ed. *Politics Canada*, 5th Edition (McGraw-Hill Ryerson 1982).

Good, David *The Politics of Anticipation: Making Canadian Federal Tax Policy* (Ottawa: School of Public Administration, Carleton University, 1980).

Government of Canada *Report Of The Committee on the Concept of the Ombudsman* (Ottawa: Supply and Services Canada, 1977).

Griffith, J.A.G. and H. Street *Principles of Administrative Law*, 3rd ed. (London: Pitman, 1963).

Hanson, A.H. and Bernard Crick, eds. *The Commons in Transition* (London: Fontana, 1970).

Hartle, Douglas "Canada's Watchdog Growing too Strong?" *The Globe and Mail* (January 10, 1979).

_____ *The Expenditure Budget Process in the Government of Canada* (Toronto: Canadian Tax Foundation, 1978).

_____ *Public Policy Decision Making and Regulation* (Montreal: Institute for Research on Public Policy, 1979).

_____ *The Revenue Budget Process of the Government of Canada: Description, Appraisal and Proposals* (Toronto: Canadian Tax Foundation 1982).

_____ "The Role of the Auditor General of Canada", *Canadian Tax Journal*, Vol. 23, No. 3.

Heady, Bruce *Cabinet Ministers* (London: Allen and Unwin, 1974).

Hockin, Thomas A., "The Advance of Standing Committees in Canada's House of Commons: 1965 to 1970", *Canadian Public Administration*, Vol. XIII, No. 2 (Summer 1970).

Hockin, Thomas A., ed., *Apex of Power* (Toronto: McGraw-Hill Ryerson, 1971).

Hodgetts, J.E. *The Canadian Public Service* (Toronto: University of Toronto Press, 1973).

Huntington, Honourable Ronald, P.C., M.P. and Claude-André Lachance, M.P. "Accountability: Closing the Loop" a paper submitted to the Special Committee of the House of Commons on Standing Orders and Procedure, November 9, 1982.

Irvine, William "Power Requires Representation", *Policy Options*, Vol. 1, No. 4, (December/January, 1980-81) pp. 20-26.

Jackson, Robert J. and Michael M. Atkinson *The Canadian Legislative System* (Toronto: Macmillan of Canada, Second Edition 1981).

Jerome, James Memorandum to Members of Parliament, Office of the Speaker of the House of Commons, Ottawa (November 10, 1978).

Jewett, Pauline "The Reform of Parliament", *Journal of Canadian Studies*, 1, (1966).

Kernaghan, Kenneth "Responsible Public Bureaucracy: A Rationale and Framework for Analysis", *Canadian Public Administration*, Vol. XVI, No. 4 (Winter 1973).

_____ "Politics, Policy and Public Servants: Political Neutrality Revisited", *Canadian Public Administration*, Vol. XIX, No. 3 (Spring 1977).

_____ *Freedom of Information and Ministerial Responsibility*, Research Publication 2 (Toronto: Commission on Freedom of Information and Individual Privacy, 1979).

_____ "Power, Parliament and Public Servants in Canada: Ministerial Responsibility Reexamined", a paper prepared for the Conference on Legislative Studies in Canada, Simon Fraser University, (Frebruary 15-17, 1979).

Kornberg, Allan *Canadian Legislative Behaviour: A Study of the 25th Parliament* (Toronto: Holt, Rinehart & Winston, 1967).

_____ "Parliament in Canadian Society", in Allan Kornberg & Lloyd D. Musolf, *Legislatures in Development Perspective*, (Durham, N.C.: Duke University Press, 1970).

_____ **and William Mishler** *Influence in Parliament: Canada* (Durham, N.C.: Duke University Press, 1976).

Kroeker, Hal V. *Accountability and Control of the Government Expenditure Process* (Montreal: C.D. Howe Research Institute, 1978).

_____ **and Douglas Hartle** *The Expenditure Budget Process in Canada* (Toronto: Canadian Tax Foundation, 1978).

Laframboise, H.L. "Administrative Reform in the Federal Public Service: Signs of a Saturation Psychosis", *Canadian Public Administration*, Vol. XIV, No. 3 (Fall 1972).

Lalonde, Marc "The Changing Role of the Prime Minister's Office", a paper presented to the 23rd Annual Meeting of the Institute of Public Administration of Canada (September 8, 1971).

Laundy, Philip "Procedures Reform in the Canadian House of Commons," *The Parliamentarian*, 50, (1969).

Lovink, J.A.A. "Parliamentary Reform and Governmental Effectiveness in Canada", *Canadian Public Administration*, No. 16 (Spring 1973).

Macdonald, Donald S. "Change in the House of Commons—New Rules", *Canadian Public Administration*, No. 13 (Spring 1970).

Macdonald, Flora "The Minister and the Mandarins" *Policy Options*, 1981, pp. 29-36.

Macguigan, Mark, P.C., M.P. "Parliamentary Reform: Impediments to an

Enlarged Role of the Backbencher", *Legislative Studies Quarterly*, III, (November 4, 1978).

Macintosh, John P. "Reform of the House of Commons: The Case of Specialization", in G. Lowenberg, ed., *Modern Parliaments: Change or Decline?*, (Chicago: Aldine-Atherton, 1971).

_____ "The Future of Representative Parliamentary Democracy", W.A.W. Neilson and J.C. MacPherson, eds., *The Legislative Process in Canada: The Need for Reform* (Montreal: Institute for Research on Public Policy, 1978).

Mallory, J.R. "The Uses of Legislative Committees" *Canadian Public Administration.* Vol. VI, No. 1 (Spring 1963).

_____ "The Minister's Office Staff: An Unreformed Part of the Public Service", *Canadian Public Administration*, Vol. X, No. 1 (Spring 1967).

_____ "Parliamentary Scrutiny of Delegated Legislation in Canada: A Large Step Forward and a Small Step Back", *Public Law*, 1972.

_____ **and B.A. Smith** "The Legislative Role of Parliamentary Committees in Canada: The Case of the Joint Committee on the Public Service Bills", *Canadian Public Administration*, Vol. XV, No. 1 (Spring 1972).

_____ "Responsive and Responsible Government", Transactions of the Royal Society of Canada, Series IV, Vol. XII (1974).

Marshall, Geoffrey and Graeme C. Moodie *Some Problems of Constitution*, 4th rev. ed. (London: Hutchinson, 1967).

Maslove, Allan "Tax Expenditures: the Other Side of Government Spending", in Bruce Doern and Allan Maslove eds. *The Public Evaluation of Government Spending* (Montreal: Institute for Research on Public Policy, 1979) pp. 149-168.

Matheson, W.A. *The Prime Minister and the Cabinet* (Toronto: Methuen, 1976).

Meekison, J.P. ed. *Canadian Federalism: Myth or Reality, Third Edition*, (Toronto: Methuen, 1977).

Meisel, John "Citizen Demands and Government Response", *Canadian Public Policy*, Vol. II, No. 2 (Autumn 1976).

Mendel, Francoise, ed. *Parliaments of the World*, (London: Macmillan, 1976).

Neilson, William A. and James C. Macpherson, eds. *The Legislative Process in Canada: The Need for Reform* (Montreal: Institute for Research on Public Policy, 1978).

Pantich, Leo, ed. *The Canadian State* (Toronto: University of Toronto Press, 1977).

Pridd, Richard W. and G. Bruce Doern *The Politics and Management of Canadian Economic Policy* (Toronto: Macmillan of Canada, 1978).

Presthos, Robert *Elites in the Policy Process* (London: Cambridge University Press, 1974).

_____ *Accommodation in Canadian Politics* (Toronto: Macmillan of Canada, 1973).

The Prime Minister's Office Prime Minister's Office Budget and Man Years (Ottawa: 1979).

Prince, Michael "The Policy Advisory Units in Government Departments", in G. Bruce Doern and Peter Aucoin, eds. *Canadian Public Policy: Organization, Process and Management* (Toronto: Macmillan of Canada, 1979).

Pross, Paul, ed. *Pressure Group Behaviour in Canadian Politics* (Toronto: McGraw-Hill Ryerson, 1975).

Public Service Commission of Canada *Public Service and Public Interest*, (Ottawa: Supply and Services Canada, 1978).

Punnett, R.M. *British Government & Politics* (London: Heinemann, 1970).

_____ *The Prime Minister in Canadian Government and Politics*, (Toronto: Macmillan of Canada, 1977).

Radwanski, George *Trudeau* (Toronto: Macmillan of Canada, 1977).

Reid, Gordon *The Politics of Financial Control: The Role of the House of Commons* (London: Hutchison, 1966).

Reid, John, M.P. "The Backbencher and the Discharge of Legislative Responsibilities" in W.A.W. Neilson and J.C. MacPherson eds., *The Legislative Process in Canada: The Need for Reform*, (Montreal: Institute for Research on Public Policy, 1978).

Ridley, F.F. "Responsibility and the Official: Forms and Ambiguities", *Government and Opposition*, Vol. 10, No. 4 (Autumn 1975).

Robert, Honourable John, Secretary of State *Legislation on Public Access to Government Documents*, (Ottawa: Supply and Services Canada, 1977).

Robinson, Ann *Parliament and Public Spending* (London: Heinemann, 1979).

Roche, Douglas D. *The Human Side of Politics* (Toronto: Clarke, Irwin, 1976).

Rosen, Phillip *Delegated Legislation in a Parliamentary System*, (Ottawa: Library of Parliament, 1977).

Rowley, J.W. and Stanbury, W.T. eds. *Competition Policy in Canada: Stage II, Bill C-13* (Montreal: Institute for Research on Public Policy, 1978).

Royal Commission on Financial Management and Accountability *Final Report* (Ottawa: Supply and Services Canada, 1979)

Rush, Michael "The Development of the Committee System in the Canadian House of Commons—Reassessment and Reform", *The Parliamentarian*, No. 55 (July 1974).

_____ "The Development of the Committee System in the Canadian House of Commons—Diagnosis & Revitalization", *The Parliamentarian*, No. 55 (July 1974).

Second Report of the Standing Joint Committee of the Senate and of the

House of Commons on Regulations and Other Statutory Instruments
Second Session of the Thirtieth Parliament, 1976-77 (Ottawa: Supply
and Services Canada, 1977).

Select Committee on Procedures *First Report, Session 1977-78* (London:
H.M.S.O., 1978).

Self, Peter *Administrative Theories and Politics* (London: George Allen and
Unwin, 1972).

Simpson, Geoffrey *Discipline & Power* (Toronto: Personal Library
Publishers, 1980).

Simeon, R. *Federal-Provincial Diplomacy: The Making of Recent Policy in
Canada* (Toronto: University of Toronto Press, 1972).

_____ "The 'Overload Thesis' and Canadian Government", *Canadian
Public Policy*, Vol. II, No. 2 (Autumn 1976).

Sinclair, Sonja *Cordial but not Cosy: A History of the Auditor General*
(Toronto: McClelland and Stewart, 1979).

Smiley, D. *Canada in Question: Federalism in the Seventies* (Toronto:
McGraw-Hill Ryerson, 1976).

_____ "Federalism and the Legislative Process in Canada in W.A.S.
Neilson and J.C. MacPherson eds., *The Legislative Process in Canada: The
Need for Reform* (Montreal: Institute for Research on Public Policy, 1978).

Smith, Bruce L.R. and D.C. Hague, eds. *The Dilemma of Accountability in
Modern Government* (London: Macmillan, 1971).

Smith, Denis "President and Parliament: The Transformation of Parliamentary Government in Canada", Thomas A. Hockin, ed., in *Apex of Power*,
(Toronto: McGraw-Hill Ryerson, 1971).

Stanbury, Honourable Richard J., Q.C. *Liberal Party of Canada — An Interpretation* (Ottawa: 1969).

Stanbury, W.T. "Lobbying and Interest Group Representation in the Legislative Process", W.A.W. Neilson and J.C. MacPherson, eds., *The Legislative
Process in Canada: The Need for Reform*, (Montreal: Institute for Research
on Public Policy, 1978).

_____ *Government Regulation: Scope Growth, Process*, (Montreal:
Institute for Research on Public Policy 1980).

Stanfield, Honourable Robert L. "The Present State of the Legislative
Process in Canada: Myths and Realities", W.A.W. Neilson and J.C. Mac-
Pherson, *The Legislative Process in Canada: The Need for Reform*,
(Montreal: Institute for Research on Public Policy, 1978).

Stanyer, Jeffrey and Brian Smith *Administering Britain* (Glasgow: Fontana/
Collins, 1976).

Stevens, Geoffrey "The Influence and Responsibilties of the Media in the
Legislative Process", W.A.W Neilson and J.C. MacPherson, eds., *The
Legislative Process in Canada: The Need for Reform*, (Montreal: Institute
for Research on Public Policy, 1978).

Steward, John "Spending the Tax Dollars", *Canadian Tax Journal*, Vol. XIX, No. 4 (July-August 1971).

Stewart, John B. *The Canadian House of Commons: Procedure and Reform* (Montreal and London: McGill-Queen's University Press, 1977).

Tellier, Paul "Pour une Réforme des Cabinets de Ministres Fédéraux", *Canadian Public Administration*, Vol. II, No. 4 (Winter 1968).

The Task Force on Canadian Unity *A Future Together* (Ottawa: Supply and Services Canada, 1979).

Thomas, Paul G. "Parliament and the Purse Strings", A study prepared for the Royal Commission on Financial Management and Accountability, Ottawa (1977).

_____ **and P.C. Dobell** "Parliament and the Control of Public Expenditure", a report to the Royal Commission on Financial Management and Accountability (Ottawa: 1977).

Tupper, Allan and G. Bruce Doern, ed. *Public Corporations and Public Policy in Canada* (Montreal: Institute for Research on Public Policy, 1981).

VanLoon, R.J. and M. Whittington *The Canadian Political System*, 3rd ed. (Toronto: McGraw-Hill Ryerson, 1981).

Walkland, S.A. and Michael Ryle, eds. *The Commons in the 70s* (London: Fontana, 1976).

Ward, Norman "A Canadian Committee on Estimates", *Parliamentary Affairs*, 10, (1956-57).

_____ "The Committee on Estimates", *Canadian Public Administration*, Vol. VI, No. 7 (March 1963).

_____ *The Public Purse* (Toronto: University of Toronto Press, 1964).

Williams, Blair "The Para-Political Bureaucracy in Ottawa", a paper prepared for the Conference on Legislative Studies in Canada, Simon Fraser University, Vancouver, B.C. (February 1979).

Wilson, Vincent Seymour *Canadian Public Policy and Public Administration: Theory and Environment* (Toronto: McGraw-Hill Ryerson, 1981).

Zussman, David "The Image of the Public Service in Canada", *Canadian Public Administration*, Vol. 25, No. 1 (Spring 1982).

The Business Council on National Issues was formed in 1976 and is now composed of 150 leading Canadian corporations. The organization is the means by which business leaders have chosen to contribute personally to the development of public policy and to the shaping of national priorities.

The Business Council seeks to foster public policies which will achieve sound economic growth, improved employment opportunities, a healthier, more vibrant competitive sector, and social and political initiatives which will enhance the well-being of Canadians. Members of the Council believe that the interests of business and the interests of all Canadians are frequently parallel, and that a sound appreciation by the public and the private sectors of one another's perspectives will benefit our country.

The Business Council has three distinctive features: it comprises solely chief executive officers of member corporations; it covers the full range of industry, trade, commerce and finance; and it devotes itself to developing positions on a limited number of public policies of national significance. The personal involvement of chief executives provides the broad perspective needed for constructive dialogue and the breadth of experience necessary to develop realistic and useful positions. The members are able to draw on their corporate staff resources which, combined with studies by independent research groups commissioned by the Business Council, enables them to address effectively a diverse range of issues.

A major part of the work of the Business Council is carried out under the direction of task forces established to deal with particular areas of concern. Composed of council members, these task forces are usually chaired by members of the Policy Committee. They are formed, reshaped and dissolved as circumstances dictate or their work is completed.

The Business Council also works to improve dialogue and to lessen confrontation among major groups in Canadian society. Toward this end, it maintains continuing liaison with governments and their agencies, with leaders of organized labour, with a variety of interest groups, and with other business organizations.